HUDSON HERITAGE

An Artist's Perspective on Architecture

KARL BECKWITH SMITH III

Salmagundi Press
COLD SPRING, NEW YORK

Hudson Heritage
An Artist's Perspective on Architecture
Copyright © 1989 by Salmagundi Press, Ltd.
Illustration Copyright © 1989 by Karl Beckwith Smith III
Graphic Production by Charlotte Krebs
Typeset in Goudy Old Style
All rights reserved.
This book, or any portion thereof,
may not be reproduced in any form without
permission in writing from the publisher.
Published by Salmagundi Press, Ltd.
66 Main Street, Cold Spring, NY 10516
Printed by Worzalla, Stevens Point, WI
First edition: 1989

Library of Congress Cataloging in Publication Data
Smith, Karl Beckwith III, 1950 -
Hudson Heritage: An Artist's Perspective on Architecture
ISBN 0-9622509-0-2

INTRODUCTION

"Architecture is the most unselfish of the arts, it belongs to passers-by and every old house and garden....is a gift to the nation, to be enjoyed by future generations who will learn from it more of history and art and philosophy than may be found in books."

From "On the Making of Gardens"
by George Sitwell

There are many ways of looking at architecture, past and present. The antiquarian's search for the relics of the past, the historian's study of the facts associated with places and their importance, the collector's loving attention to artifact and the aesthete's contemplation of form and beauty are all valid and productive approaches. Karl Beckwith Smith III has chosen to record the architecture of the Hudson Valley by drawing selected historic buildings, from Westchester to Albany, from a perspective that draws on these several ways of looking at the subject and filters them through the individual artist's eye.

His chronology is drawn from two hundred years of New York history, from 1700 to 1900. In these drawings a group of diverse properties are woven together into a rich tapestry of images.

Boscobel is pleased to host the opening exhibition of Hudson Heritage: An Artist's Perspective on Architecture and to bring the work to the attention of an interested public. Awareness of our architectural heritage is the first important step toward involvement in historic preservation.

Frederick W. Stanyer
Executive Director
Boscobel Restoration, Inc.

PREFACE

Architecture is an art form that inevitably touches us all. It starts at home: our dwellings are our most important possessions and expressions of ourselves. In all my years of travelling around the Hudson Valley, I have rarely met anybody who has not been totally agreeable to talking about his or her house to an interested stranger. If it is an old house, just about every owner has developed a personal idea of its history or devised a theory (often quite elaborate) about its changing nature. As social animals, we also have a compelling interest in what other people's houses contain and/or express and how they compare to our own. By extension, we view all other architecture we encounter (civic, commercial, religious, etc.) in relation to our homes. Because of this abiding, intimate association we have with the buildings in which we live, work, worship or pay our taxes, we are also drawn to historic architecture, and the mysteries created by the distance of time only make them all the more tantalizing.

A new pictorial book on historic Hudson Valley architecture is always a cause for celebration. It will undoubtedly contain images we recognize, rekindling our affections for favorite buildings, like old friends, or triggering memories of past encounters. There are certain houses you can never see too often: each updated view, new perspective or individual artistic interpretation adds to our appreciation of the building and the history it represents. Then, too, such a book is always guaranteed to introduce us to a new building or two that will thrill our sense of discovery or pique our insatiable historical curiosity. As I can testify, you can never count on mastering the subject. Just as you grow confident in your understanding of a house, an area, a period or a style, you are humbled by a revelation -- often from a picture in a book -- that causes you to revise your assumptions about them.

Karl Beckwith Smith III has created an engrossing book of pictures of historic buildings in the Hudson Valley. In his pen and ink wash drawings of many of the region's architectural icons, he combines the expressive hand of an artist, the documentary detail of a historian, and the fervor of a preservationist to create direct but sensitive images of these richly evocative buildings. Each image speaks for itself in Mr. Smith's cool, draughtsmanly style, yet their particular collection in this book, with supporting captions, is integral to their presentation, for Karl Smith is as concerned with engendering our commitment to these buildings and their histories as he is with the appeal of his art. In the artist's view, these buildings are not just objects of history but history itself; living landmarks in a changing cultural landscape that give us reference points to understand our past and appreciate our place in the present.

An artist's view can capture the spirit (or perhaps even spirits!) of an old building and give us insight into the expressive character of the place. Our history can be preserved in mediums other than artifacts and presented in forms other than scholarly (or promotional) prose. I, for one, am excited by the resurgence of interest in the Hudson Valley in the visual arts and creative literature. Recent creative works like T.C. Boyle's bestselling novel *World's End,* John Hulsey's bold riverscapes, or John Novi's extraordinary cuisine are all concerned with the history and the idea of history in the Hudson Valley. They all give us a vivid, sensual experience of the place. With his book of pictures, Karl Beckwith Smith joins ranks with our creative historians.

Neil Larson
Troy, New York

ARTIST'S PREFACE TO THE FIRST EDITION

The idea for this book grew out of a series of fifty drawings of historic buildings in the Hudson Valley that I completed during 1988 and 1989. When all of the drawings came together they began to tell a story. It was possible to draw comparisons between them and, through them, begin to unravel the rich and varied tapestry that is the history of Hudson Valley architecture. It was apparent that history, as well as art, was the subject and so the drawings evolved into a book with notes.

Architecture is a primary expression of the relationship between man and nature. This relationship is revealed not only in man's choice of materials and in his craftsmanship, but also in the manner and style in which he puts these things together. When Europeans first came to the new world they lived in log huts with dirt floors. Wooden floors, window glazing and chimneys later appeared as signs the settlers were conquering and taming the wilderness. Eventually their living structures became more than mere protection from the elements and the Indians.

The Hudson River Valley was the cradle and cauldron of a new civilization on a new continent. In time, mechanization enabled people to enjoy elaborate architecture and furnishings; leisure allowed them to develop and enjoy the extraordinary landscape of their region.

In these drawings I have tried to maintain a consistent vision, through control of the techniques of pen and ink wash, that will allow the viewer to enjoy the diversity of the architecture as well as the art. I have tried to convey something of the essence of each place through the lighting, the expression of the time of day it was drawn, the season, weather and siting.

I wanted the buildings to suggest questions about how they were built, who lived in them, what daily life was like during successive periods of habitation and how this affected the architecture and, finally, what was the relationship of the people and the architecture to the river?

In realizing the drawings there were problems of access, working solitude and weather. And there were pleasures: the travel, the fascinating past lives of these places, the gardens as well as the buildings, interesting people and the experience of the essence of the places -- the air, the light, growing things, even the birds. These drawings are the product of these influences reflected through an individual artist's creative process and eye.

K.B.S.III

1 PHILIPSBURG MANOR UPPER MILLS

The vast Philipse estate, owned by Frederick Philipse, a native of Holland, was the 18th century site of a busy grist mill and the center of a highly successful commercial enterprise. The mill and manor were built in 1682 in the Dutch Colonial style. The mill, which is driven by the waters of the Pocantico River, has been carefully restored to working order and to its appearance circa 1720-1750, the time of its greatest prosperity.

The manor house was originally the headquarters for the mill. Although administrators of the business lived there it was always more a commercial building than a residence. In the years after the Revolution and the decline of the loyalist Philipse family, it became a private home. John D. Rockefeller purchased it for Sleepy Hollow Restorations in 1940 and it was opened to the public in 1943.

This view from the east shows the wooden mill and barn and the stone manor house. The house interested me because of the warehouse-like quality, reflected in its lack of ornamentation and deep set windows, that sets it apart from more typical Dutch architecture of the time. There is a very practical, businesslike feeling about the site that speaks to the energy and determination of the 18th century men of commerce who succeeded here.

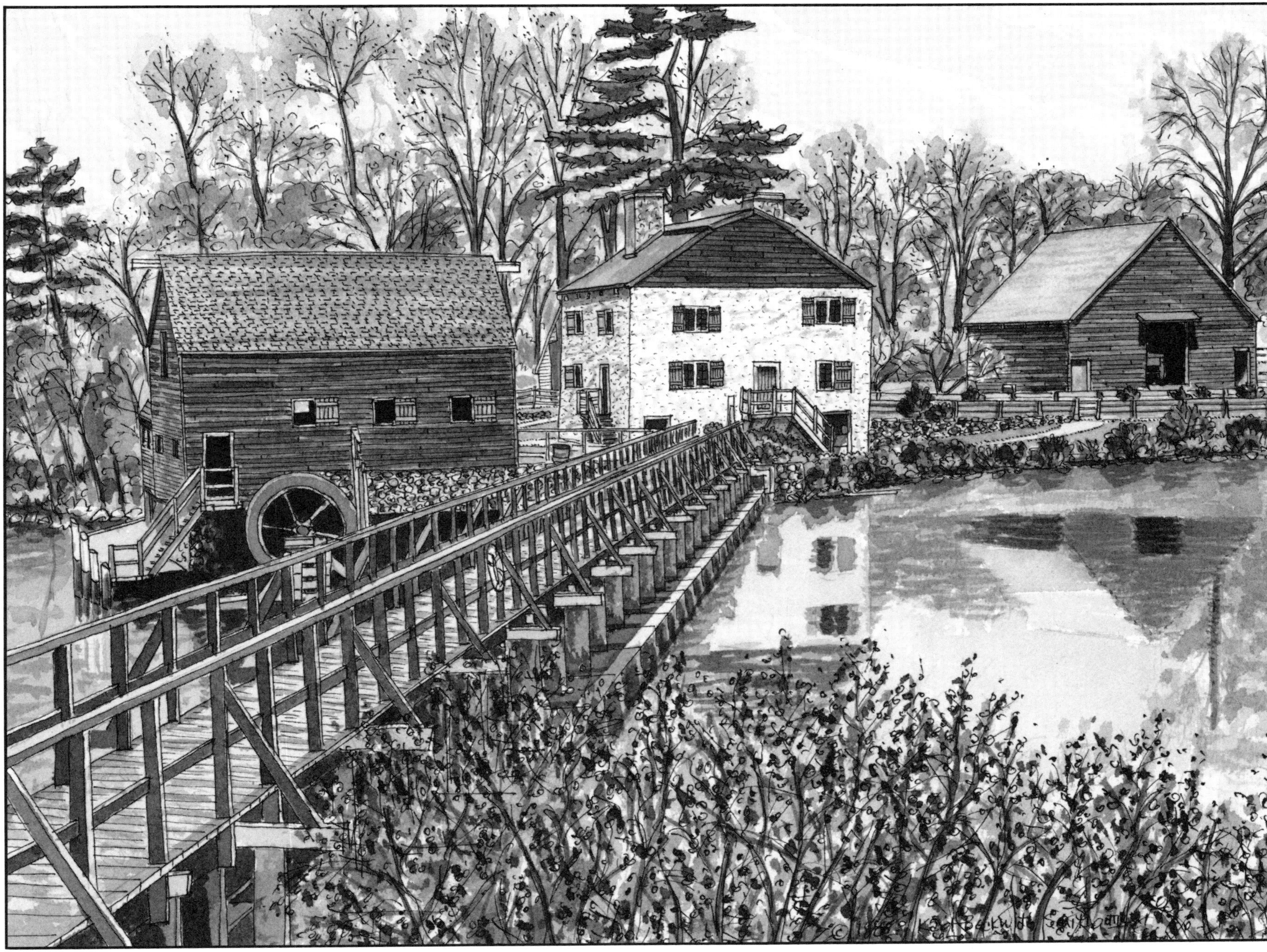

OLD DUTCH CHURCH

Frederick Philipse, owner of the 90,000 acre Manor of Philipsburg and builder of the Upper Mills, also built this fine Dutch Colonial stone church. It was constructed sometime during the 1690's and is distinguished by a beautiful bell-shaped gambrel roof. Washington Irving wrote about the church and is among the famous Americans buried in its graveyard. The southwest facade of the church offers a view of its Gothic pointed windows -- interesting early examples of the type. These giant windows give the inside of the church a very bright, airy feeling and there is special magic as the reflected leaves of the trees outside flicker in the light.

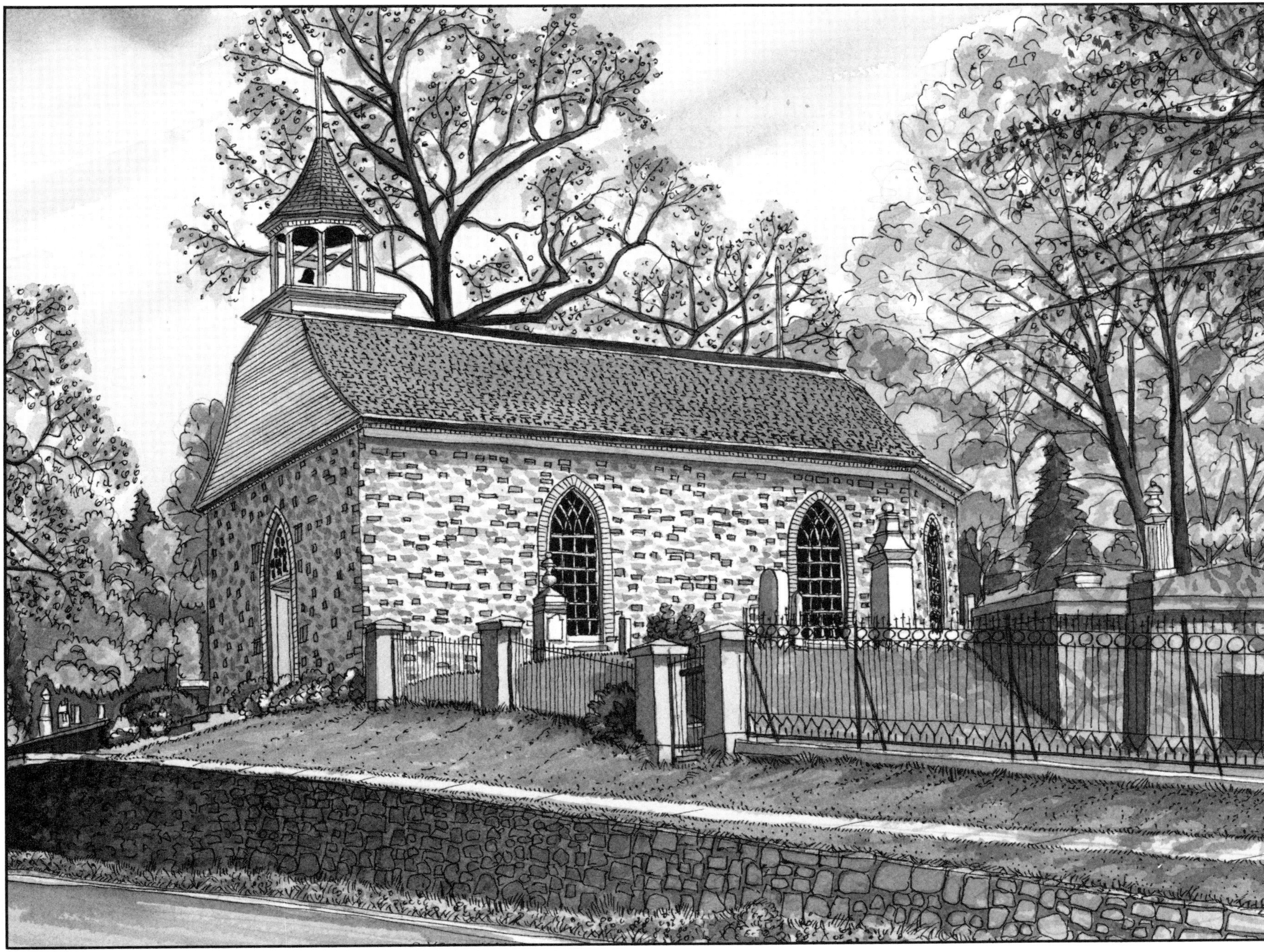

3 DeWint House

The DeWint House is the oldest standing house in Rockland County. It was build in 1700 by Daniel DeClark, a wealthy burgher, and purchased by Johannes DeWint in 1746. Constructed of local standstone and Dutch brick, it is in the Dutch style common to the architecture of New York State during the 18th century.

The two-storey house with its steeply pitched roof, imported brick and purple tiles around the fireplace was by far the most luxurious dwelling in the area. Indeed, it was luxurious enough to house the colonies' most illustrious citizen. On four separate occassions during the critical years 1780 through 1783 General George Washington stayed here. He was a guest while the fate of Tory spy Major Andre was being decided and again when the strategic plans for the evacuation of the defeated British armies were made.

When the house was acquired by the Masonic Order in 1931 it contained numerous homely articles, including furniture, andirons and kitchen utensils which had been in the house during the time of Washington's sojourn. The interior is maintained in its 18th century simplicity.

This view of the east facade shows the deep overhanging roof that served as protection from the weather before porches became a feature of domestic architecture. Some of the windows in the house contain original handmade glass.

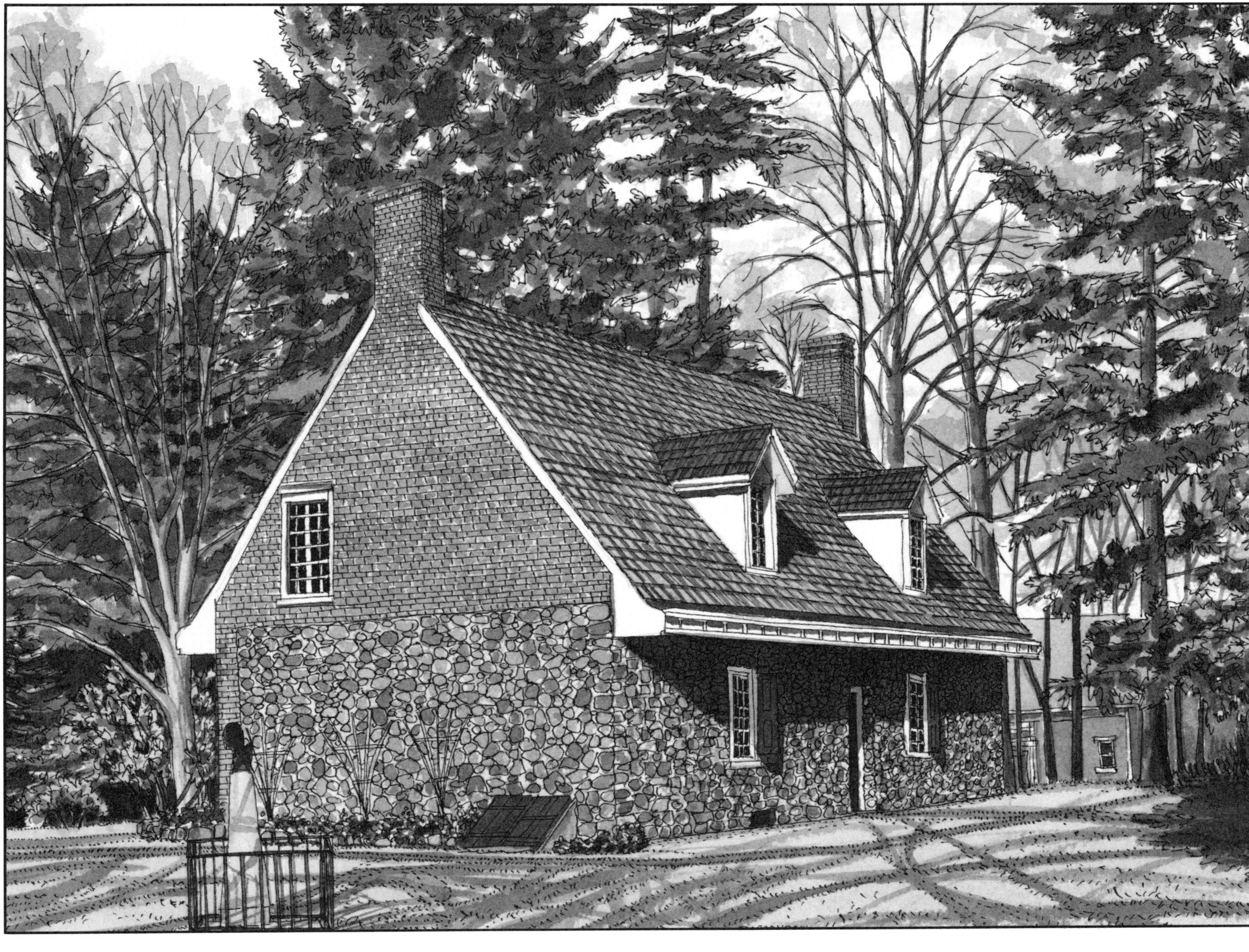

CRAILO

Crailo, which in Dutch means 'crows wood', is an early Dutch home built in 1705 by Hendrick Van Rensselaer on the vast Rensselaerswyck Manor. The house has been added to and altered many times during its almost three centuries of life. A rear wing was added in the early part of the 18th century by Van Rensselaer's son. In 1746 Crailo became a fort and gun ports were cut into its walls. In 1762 it was remodeled in the Georgian style and then, between 1783 and 1828, given Federal style mantles, windows and doorways.

Crailo was donated to the State of New York in 1924 and during the following decade was renovated to reflect its earlier Federal styling. Its 17th and 18th century artifacts, furniture and household items are a valuable record of the Dutch heritage of the Hudson Valley. Today the house is set in a riverside park and is frequented by visitors who come to enjoy scheduled demonstrations of hearth cooking and 18th century food preparation.

The view of Crailo here is of the west facade. I was especially drawn by the lovely tile roof, the diamond shaped windows and the very practical and simple wood shutters. The rhythm and placement of windows with half shutters sets this house apart from others of its type and time.

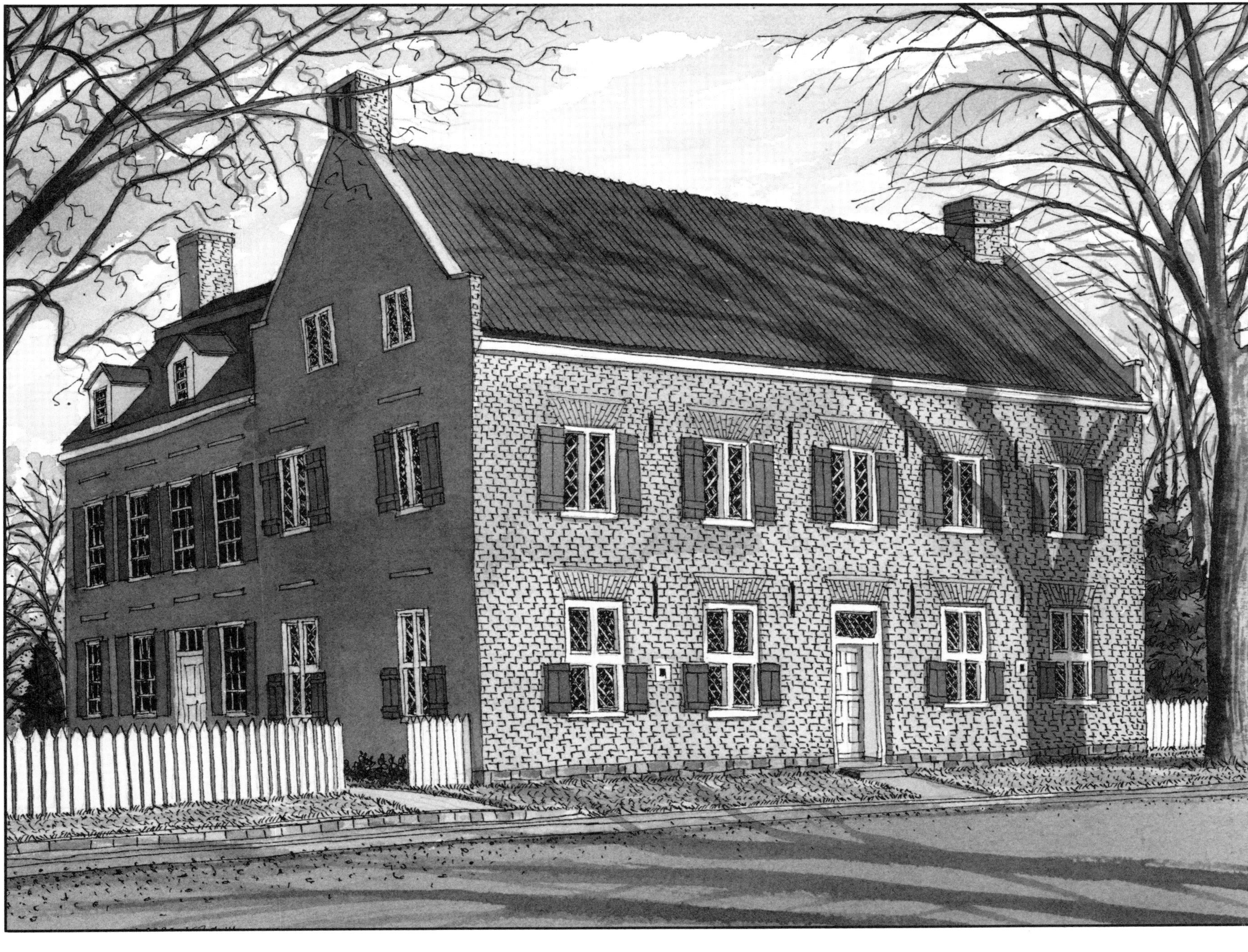

DuBois Fort

The exiled Huguenots who came to Ulster county in the last quarter of the 17th century created a community of stone dwellings built in the Medieval Flemish style of their homeland. These buildings still stand on New Paltz's Huguenot Street, the oldest street of original houses in America. The DuBois Fort, constructed in 1705 for Daniel DuBois, was originally intended as a place of retreat and safeguard - although it was never used for that purpose. Instead it became the meeting place for "The Duzine" (the twelve men who founded the community) and their descendants. Today it is a restaurant.

The south facade of the house was sketched from the street. This view includes the out-buildings associated with the house which were characteristic of the time and, I think, help give a fuller sense of time and place. DuBois was built of relatively small, pebbly gathered stones which give it textural interest.

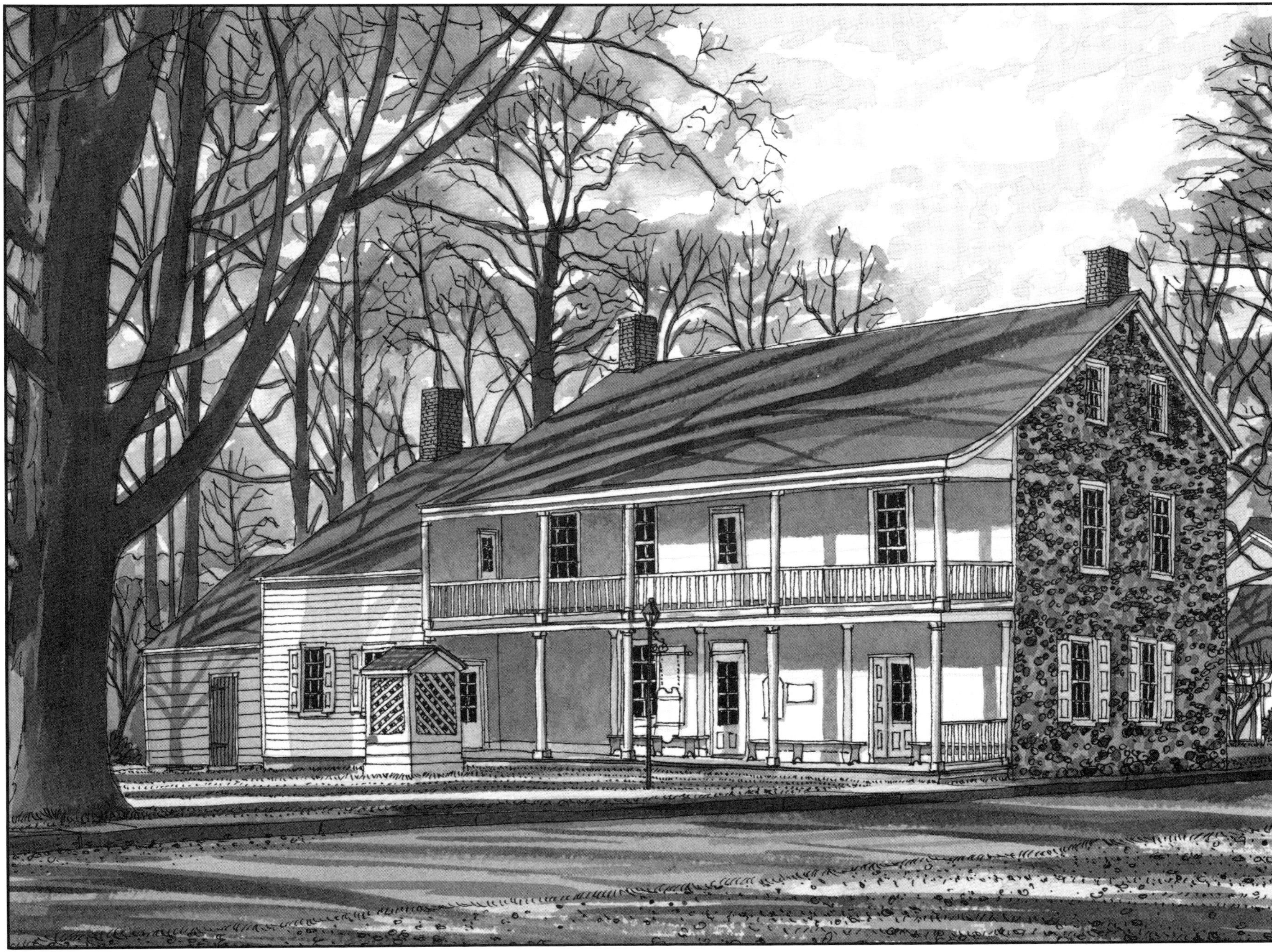

Madam Brett Homestead

This wood house in the Dutch style was built in 1709 for Catherine and Robert Brett. Madam Brett had inherited large land-holdings in Dutchess County from her father, patentee Francis Rombout, and came to Beacon to administer them. Widowed early, she successfully managed both the properties and a mill on Fishkill Creek that provided vital services to the settlers in the area.

The Brett Homestead features handmade scalloped shingles, sloped dormers and a native stone foundation. During the Revolutionary War it was used as a commissary for supplying the colonial army. Washington, Lafayette and the Baron von Steuben were among its important guests.

The Homestead has the distinction of being one of the few houses in the Hudson Valley to be continuously owned and occupied by one family for two and a half centuries. Seven generations of Brett descendants lived here until the house was purchased by Melzingah Chapter, National Society of the Daughters of the American Revolution in 1954.

The Brett Homestead is now right in the center of the city of Beacon which over the years has grown up around it. I sketched the west facade of the house to take best advantage of the light. The building is not fully restored but has been well maintained and stands as living witness to centuries of history and as a reminder of the power of memorable individuals who peopled that history.

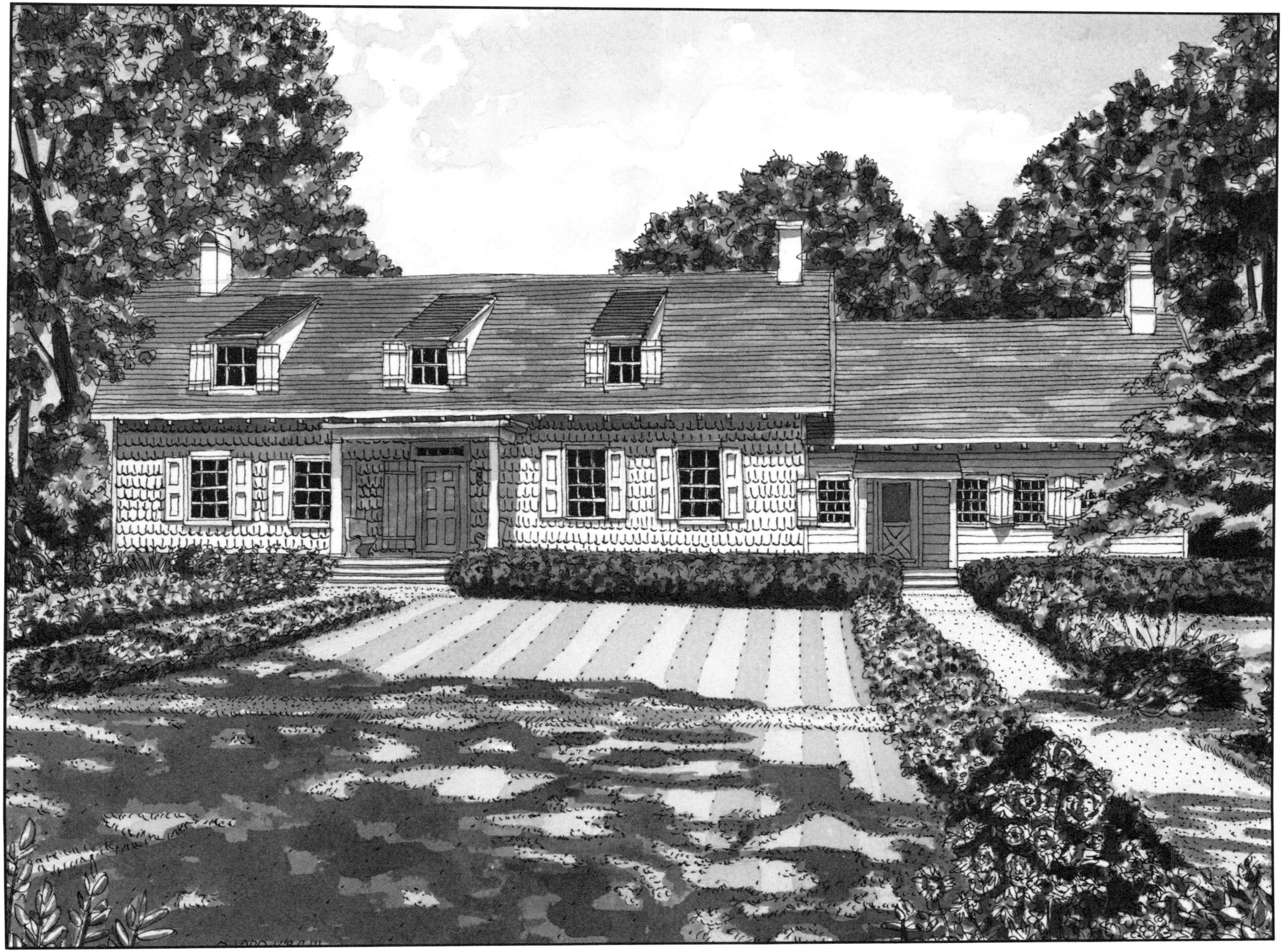

7 VAN DEUSEN HOUSE

The Jan Van Deusen House is one of twenty-five 18th century stone houses, all preserved and privately owned, in the town of Hurley. It was built in 1723. In 1777 when the state legislature was burned out of Kingston by the British the town became, for a short time, the state capital. During that time the legistature convened at the Van Deusen House, a typical Dutch-style stone house of the period.

Hurley is a time capsule of the early 18th century and this house is a little gem. It is particularly interesting to me because of its original blacksmith hardware, raised stone hitching post, and rough fieldstone construction. I chose to draw the southeast facade and thus include some of the appended buildings on the site.

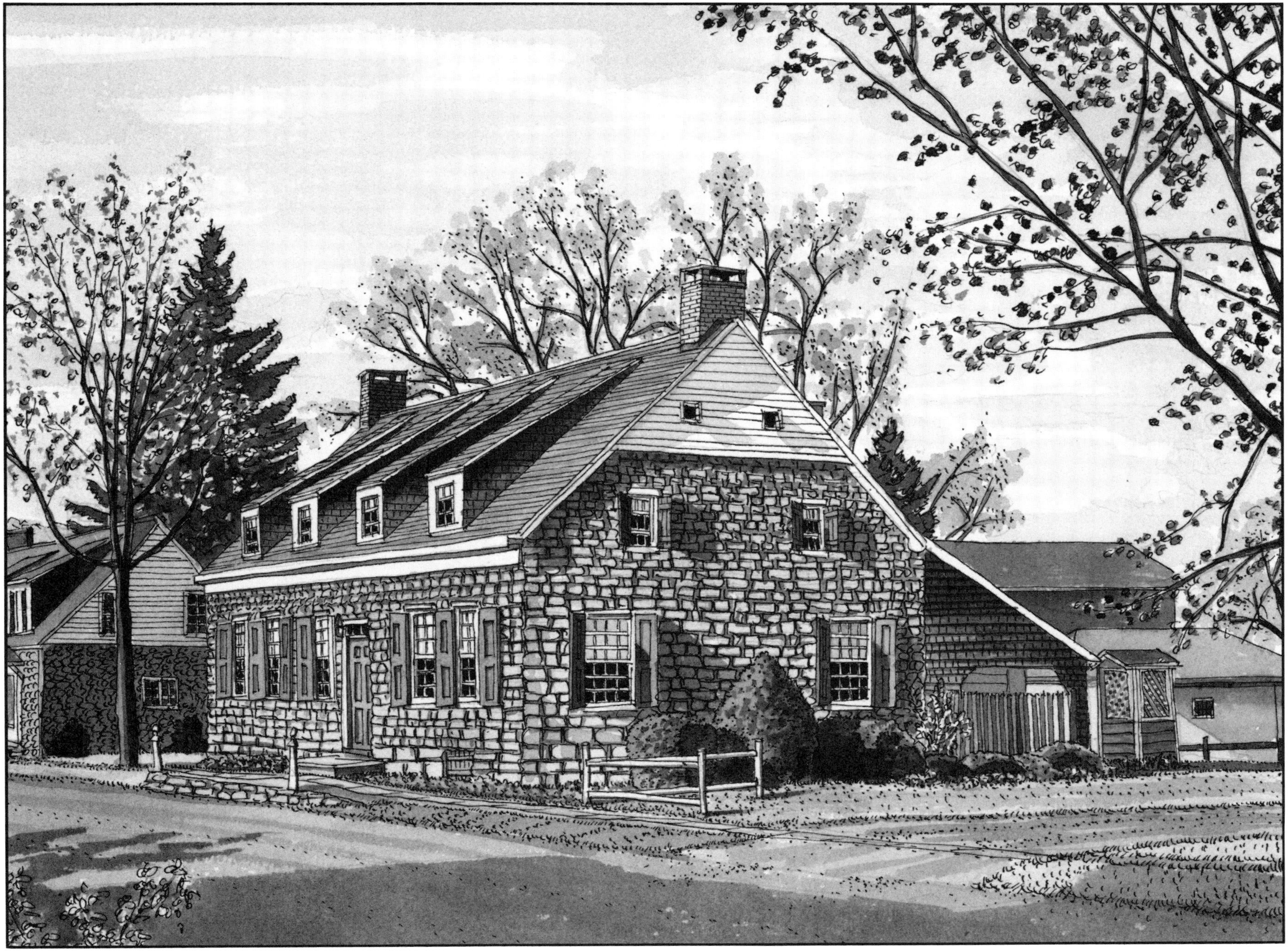

Washington's Headquarters

In 1750 Jonathan Hasbrouck purchased a small stone house in Newburgh, built a quarter of a century earlier, and began the first of a series of renovations and additions. By the beginning of the Revolutionary War the typical Dutch Huguenot house was clearly marked as the home of a successful gentleman of commerce.

As the war neared its end General Washington moved north with half his army to await, in military readiness, the negotiation of the treaty of Paris. The Hasbroucks left their home, turning it over to Washington, his wife, Martha, and several aides-de-camp who resided there from April 1782 until August 1783.

The Hasbrouck family returned to their home after Washington's departure and descendants of the family occupied it until it was purchased by the state in 1849. In 1850 Hasbrouck House, renamed Washington's Headquarters, became the first public historic site in the nation.

The drawing is of the northwest corner of the house. The dwelling, which looks like three or four typical Dutch houses under one roof, is one of the primary icons of American history. Today it is situated in a park, surrounded by the city of Newburgh, but it commands the same panoramic views of the Hudson Highlands that Washington enjoyed two centuries ago.

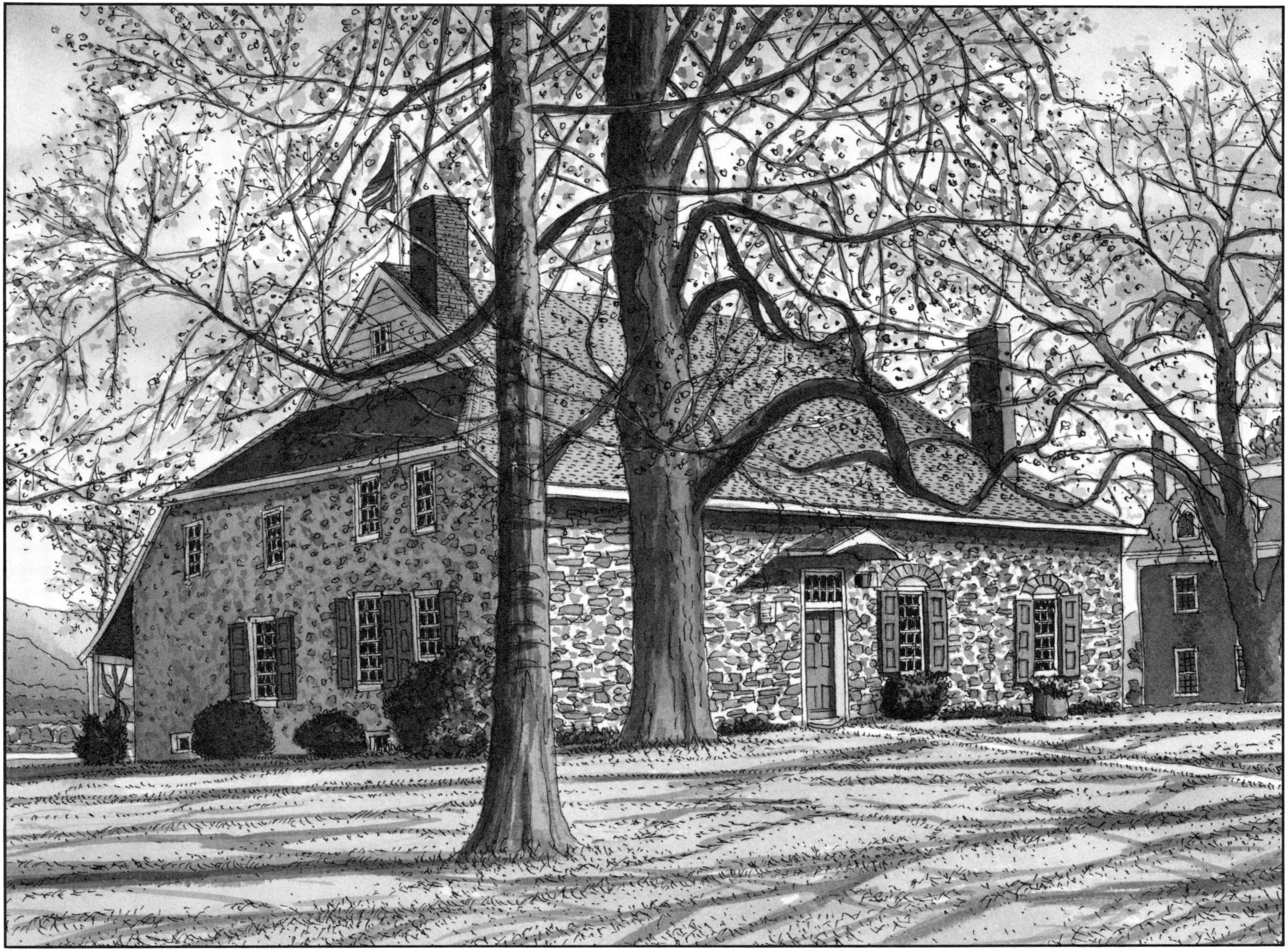

Edmonston House

This pre-revolutionary stone house is located not far from the New Windsor Cantonment, the winter encampment of the Continental Army during the final year of the revolution. William Edmonston of Ireland built the first part of the dwelling in 1755. He completed an addition to the house sometime before the war.

Edmonston House had many owners over the centuries and fell into disrepair. Structural changes were made and some of its most attractive details were obscured. In 1967 the house was purchased by The National Temple Hill Association, a local non-profit organization dedicated to restoring the Cantonment and allied historic buildings in the area. Careful restoration at Edmonston has included the replacement of 20th century windows with original style twelve over nines and the rebuilding of the masonry chimney with 18th century bricks. A blacksmith shop, believed to have been an original feature of the site, has been re-constructed and slave quarters, once located a short distance down the road, have been moved onto the property.

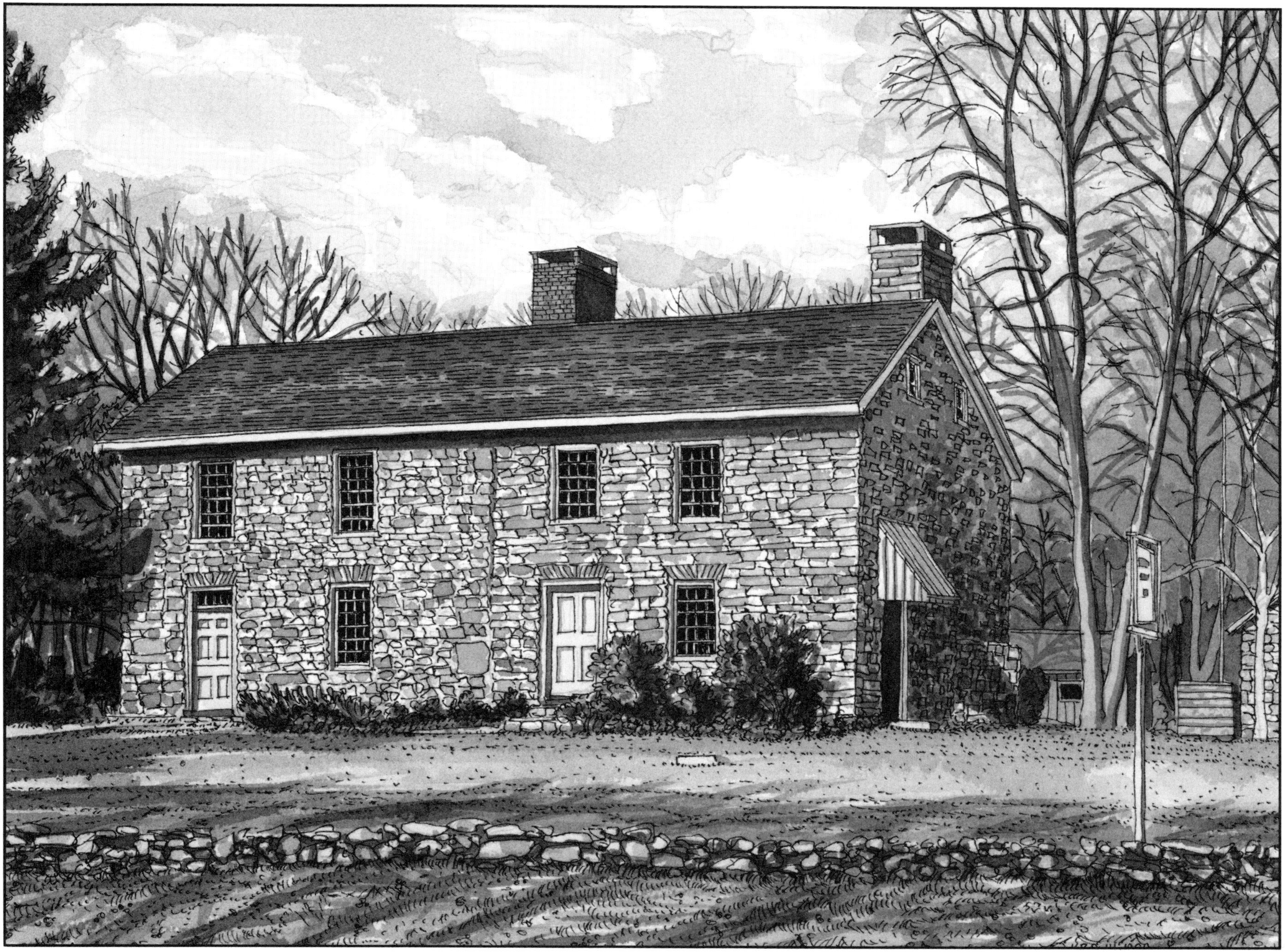

Philipse Manor Hall

Philipse Manor Hall is a Georgian style stone and brick mansion that is considered one of the finest buildings of its style in New York State. It was built in the first half of the 18th century and extensively rebuilt after 1757 by descendants of Frederick Philipse I.

In the years before the Revolution this grand home was the seat of an estate that covered almost one third of Westchester County. It was surrounded by formal gardens patterned after the exquisite planned landscapes of the English estate. After the Revolution, its loyalist owners were declared traitors by the New York State legislature and their land was confiscated and sold at auction. Philipse Manor Hall has had many owners, private and public. At one point in its history it served as the Yonkers City Hall. The building was purchased by New York State in 1908 and today houses exhibits of history, art and architecture.

The south facade shown in the drawing is the older part of the manor. The long east/west facade is now somewhat obscured by urban growth -- the manor is now a part of downtown Yonkers.

The stone work on this building is beautiful. The manor is given a more formal feeling than many stone buildings of its time by the balustrade around the top and by the very careful arrangement of the stones and the surrounding brickwork that constrains them, as in the window details.

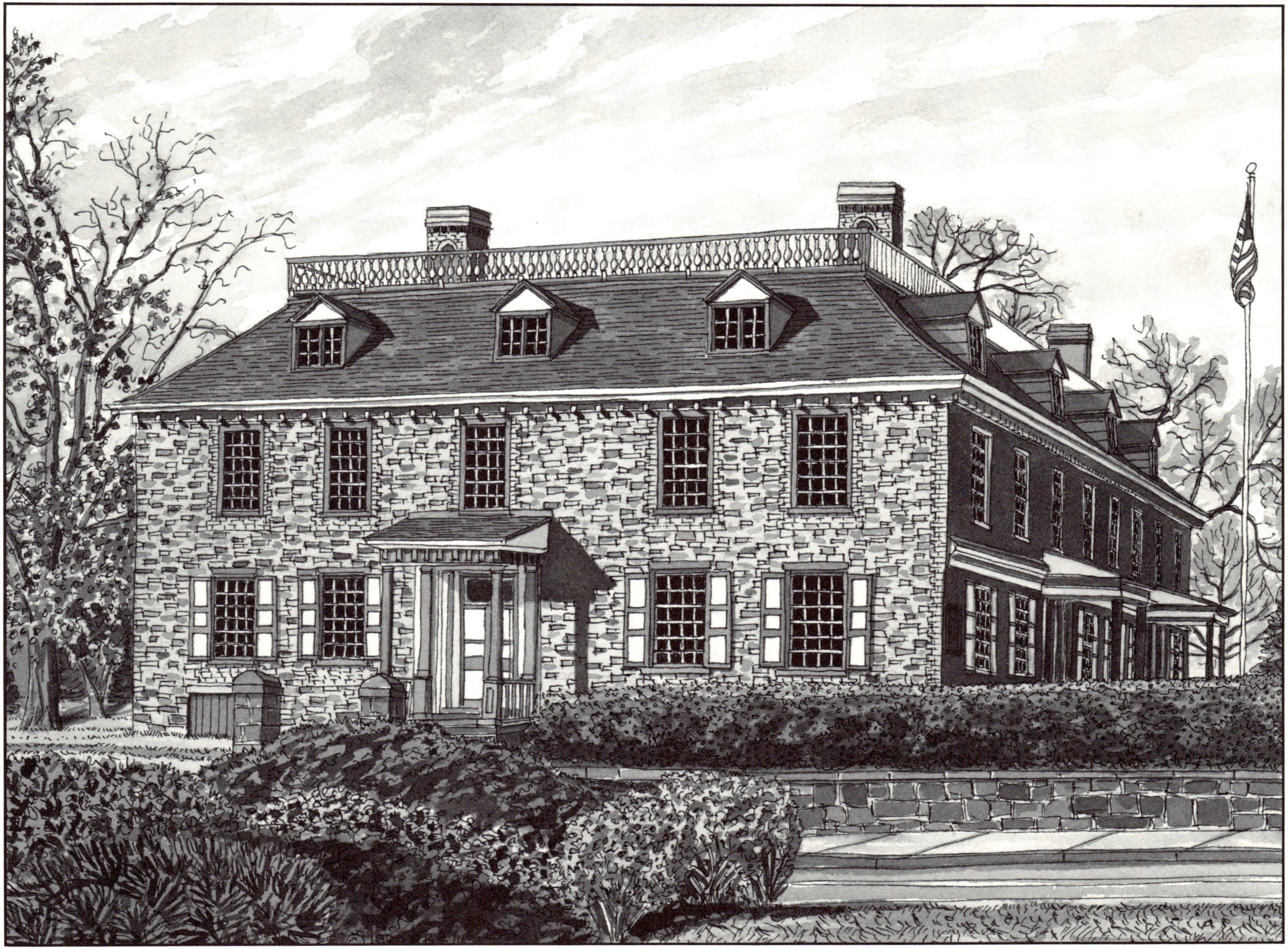

11 THE MANSE

This stone house, built in 1724, is typical of 18th century Hudson Valley Dutch Colonial architecture. The house was enlarged in 1788 and a frame wing was added about 1830. The ornamentation on the exterior was added at a later date.

The Reverend Samuel Verbryck, a friend of George Washington and co-founder of Rutgers University, was among its inhabitants. The Manse is the oldest parsonage in continuous use in the United States.

The east facade of the Manse shown here faces a green around which are other old buildings, including the church it serves. There are extensive barns and outbuildings on the north side. The Manse is a solid, comfortable house that has been maintained, but not restored, and has remained an important living part of its community.

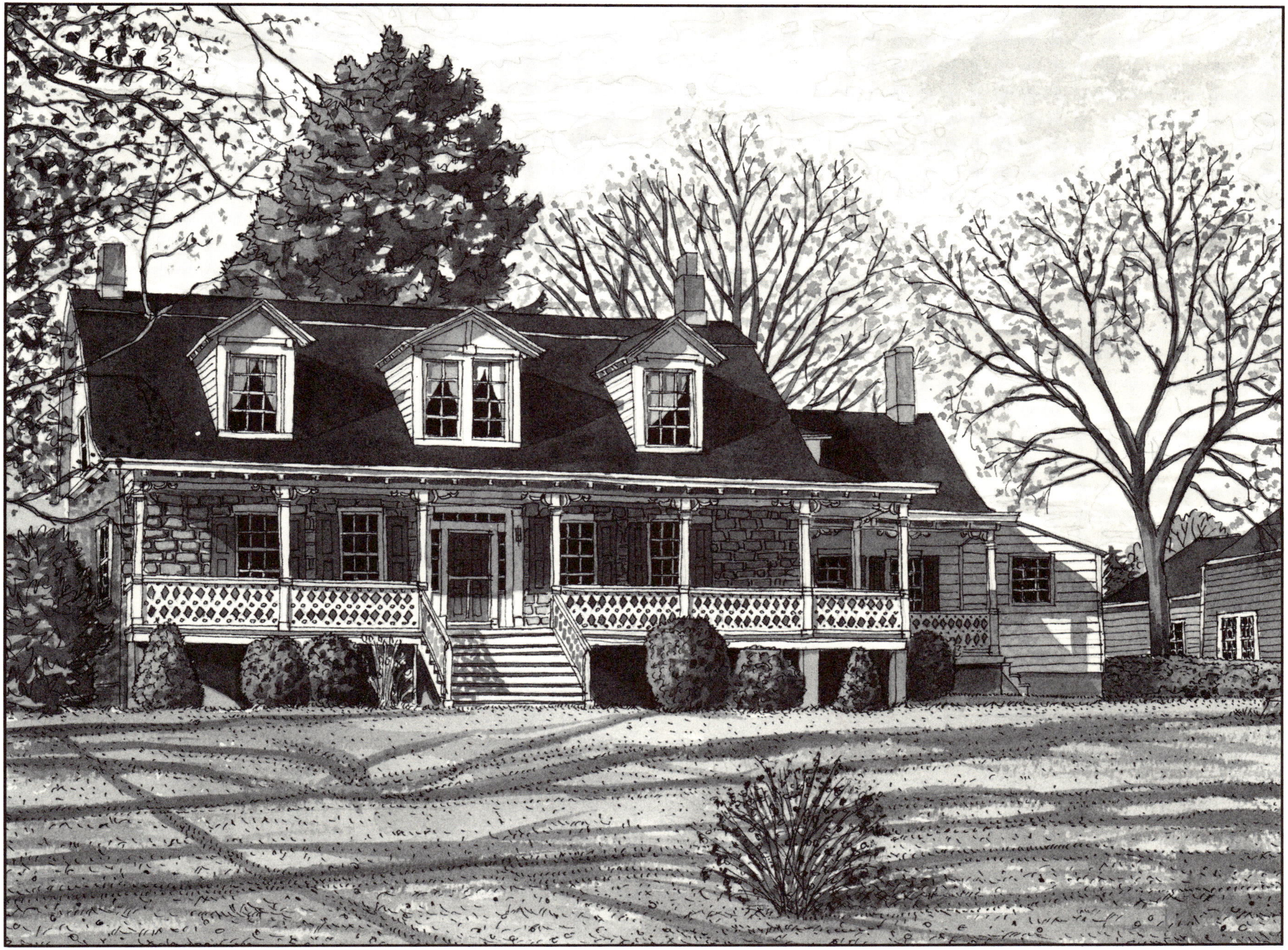

CLERMONT

Clermont was the home, from 1730 to 1962, to generations of Livingstons -- all descendants of Robert Livingston who arrived in Albany in 1675 and a decade later became first Lord of Livingston Manor, a vast holding in southern Columbia County. Livingston's son, Robert of Clermont, built the first house on the property. The house was burned to the ground by the British during the Revolution and was immediately rebuilt by Robert Livingston's daugher-in-law, and grandson, Chancellor Robert Livingston, co-drafter of the Declaration of Independence and co-inventor, with Robert Fulton, of the steamboat.

Clermont is a Georgian style stuccoed brick mansion, erected on the foundations of the house that was destroyed by fire. A north wing containing a kitchen was built in 1802; a south bedroom wing was built in 1830 and enlarged in 1893; and third floor servants' quarters with a steeply pitched slate roof were added in 1874. The house has been restored to its 1930 appearance by the State of New York which acquired it in 1962 from Alice Livingston.

I chose to draw the east facade of the house because it clearly shows the added wings and transformations of the building over time and in this way expresses the history of a family seat. The west facade faces the river and the Catskill Mountains in the distance.

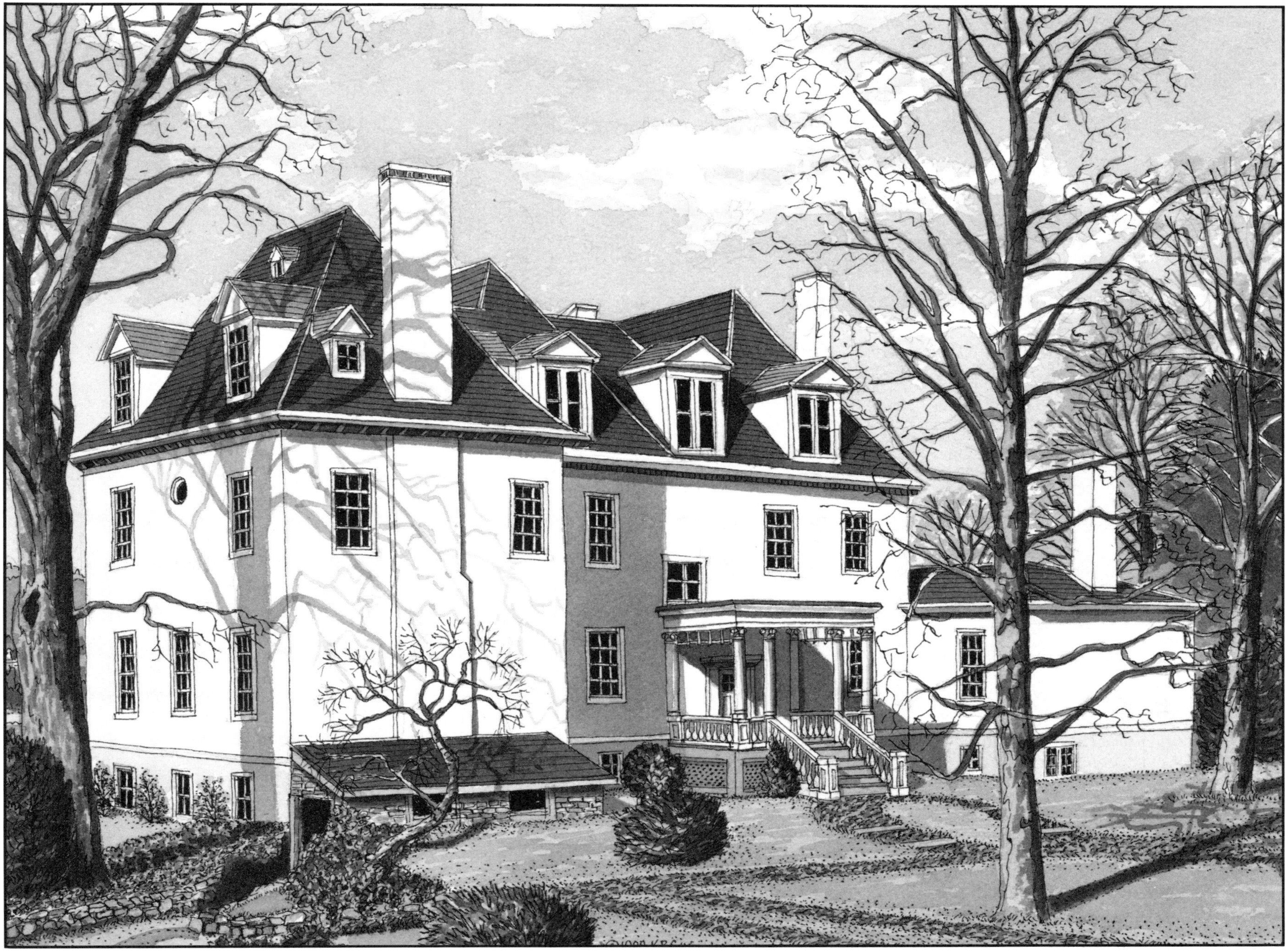

Van Wyck Homestead

The land on which the Van Wyck Homestead stands originally belonged to Madam Brett, daughter of Frances Rombout who held the 85,000 acre Rombout patent in Dutchess County. In 1732 Cornelius Van Wyck purchased almost one thousand acres from the heirs to the patent and built a three room house on the site. In 1757 he added a west wing. The house is of wood frame construction with clapboard siding and is built in the typical Dutch Colonial style.

The American Revolution placed the Van Wyck Homestead at the crossroads of history. Fishkill was a strategic point on the north-south route from Westchester to upper New York State and on the east-west line from West Point and Fort Montgomery to the New England colonies. It became the Northern Army Headquarters and Supply Depot and the Van Wyck house was requisitioned by the Continental Army as headquarters for General Putnam.

A small village was constructed around the homestead to provide housing, storage, stables, shops and vital services like blacksmithing and artillery repair. "New York Packet" publisher Samuel Loudon moved his newspaper to the Van Wyck home from British-occupied New York City and printed it here. Later, James Fenimore Cooper set scenes of his 19th century novel "The Spy" in the house.

The Van Wyck family returned to their home after the war and their descendants lived there for one hundred and fifty years. Today the house is on the National Register of Historic Places and is maintained by the Fishkill Historical Society. The view in the drawing is of the south facade of the Homestead.

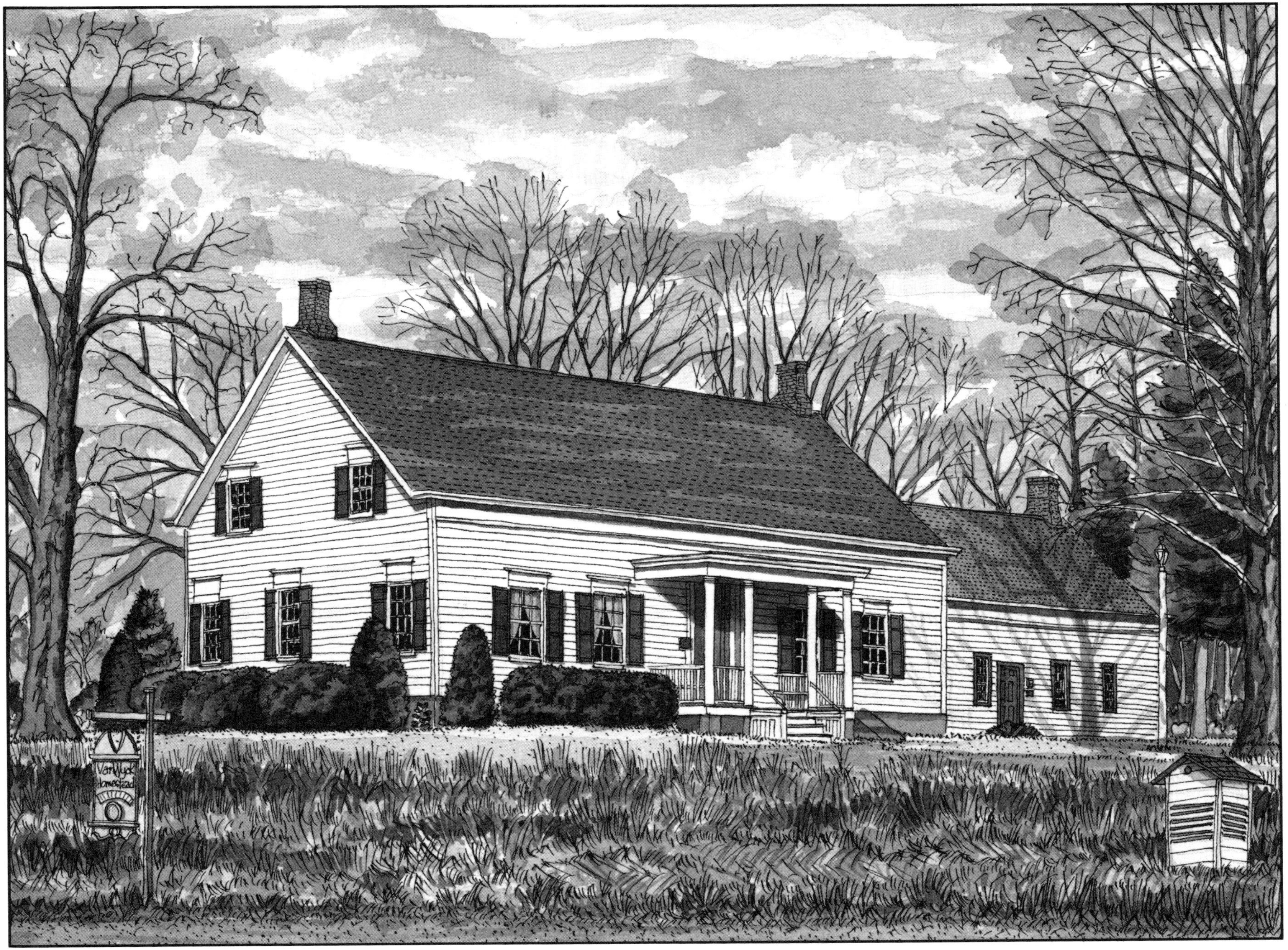

Mount Gulian

The original Dutch Colonial house erected on this site between 1730 and 1740 was built on land purchased from the Wappinger Indians in 1683. The fieldstone and wood dwelling was the headquarters of Baron von Steuben during the latter part of the Revolutionary War and was the birthplace of the Society of Cincinnati, a fraternal organization of American officers from the Continental Army whose first president was George Washington.

Mount Gulian was built for Gulian Verplank and remained in the Verplank family until 1931 when it was destroyed by fire. The present reconstruction was completed in 1976.

I found this beautifully reconstructed 18th century house hidden away behind a condominium complex just outside the city of Beacon. The house was rebuilt on its original foundation. It is situated right on the river and its lawns roll down to the river's edge. This drawing of the west facade shows the long, narrow dormers characteristic of period Hudson Valley houses and four fine chimneys that anchor the building.

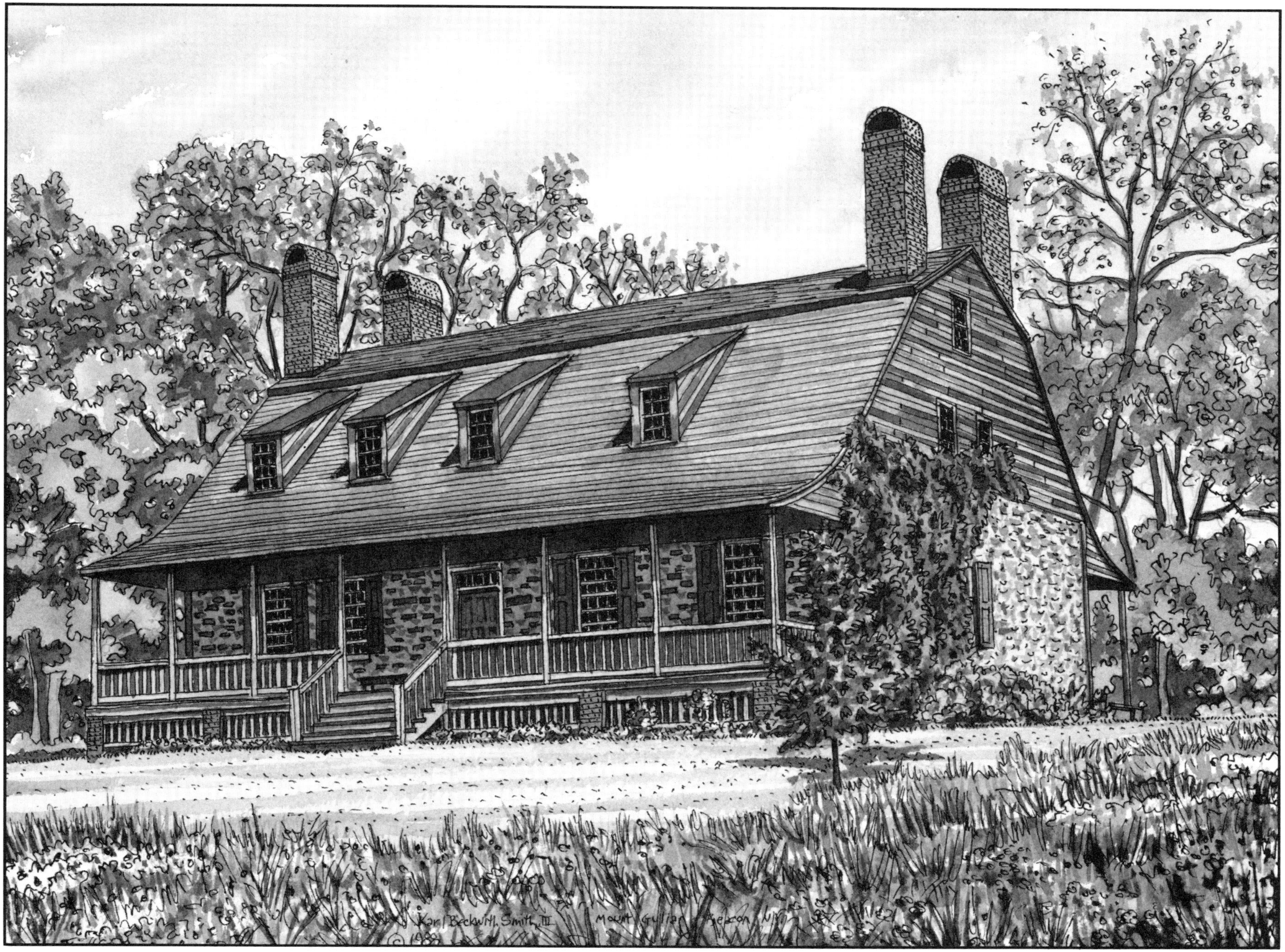
Karl Beckwith Smith, III
Mount Gulian Beacon NY
© 1988

Van Cortlandt Manor

Pierre Van Cortlandt married Joanna Livingston at the mid point of the 18th century and thus joined together two of the state's most prominent families. He built Van Cortlandt Manor in 1749. It is a stone and white clapboard house with a gracious pillared veranda on the second floor.

Joanna apparently possessed the family genes for landscaping and gardening. She is credited with designing the 750 foot, brick-paved "Long Walk" from the Manor to the Ferry House, an inn on the property. The walk is bordered by lovely gardens and its terminus is a comfortable resting place with bar and dormitory quarters once used by wayfarers on their journeys from the Croton River up the Old Albany Post Road.

Descendants of the Van Cortlandt family lived in the house for two centuries. In 1945 it was purchased by Sleepy Hollow Restorations and today is an Historic Hudson Valley site.

I have drawn the south facade of the house which faces the Croton River at the point where it flows into the Hudson. This view shows the manor's interesting combination of solid stone core and light wood verandas.

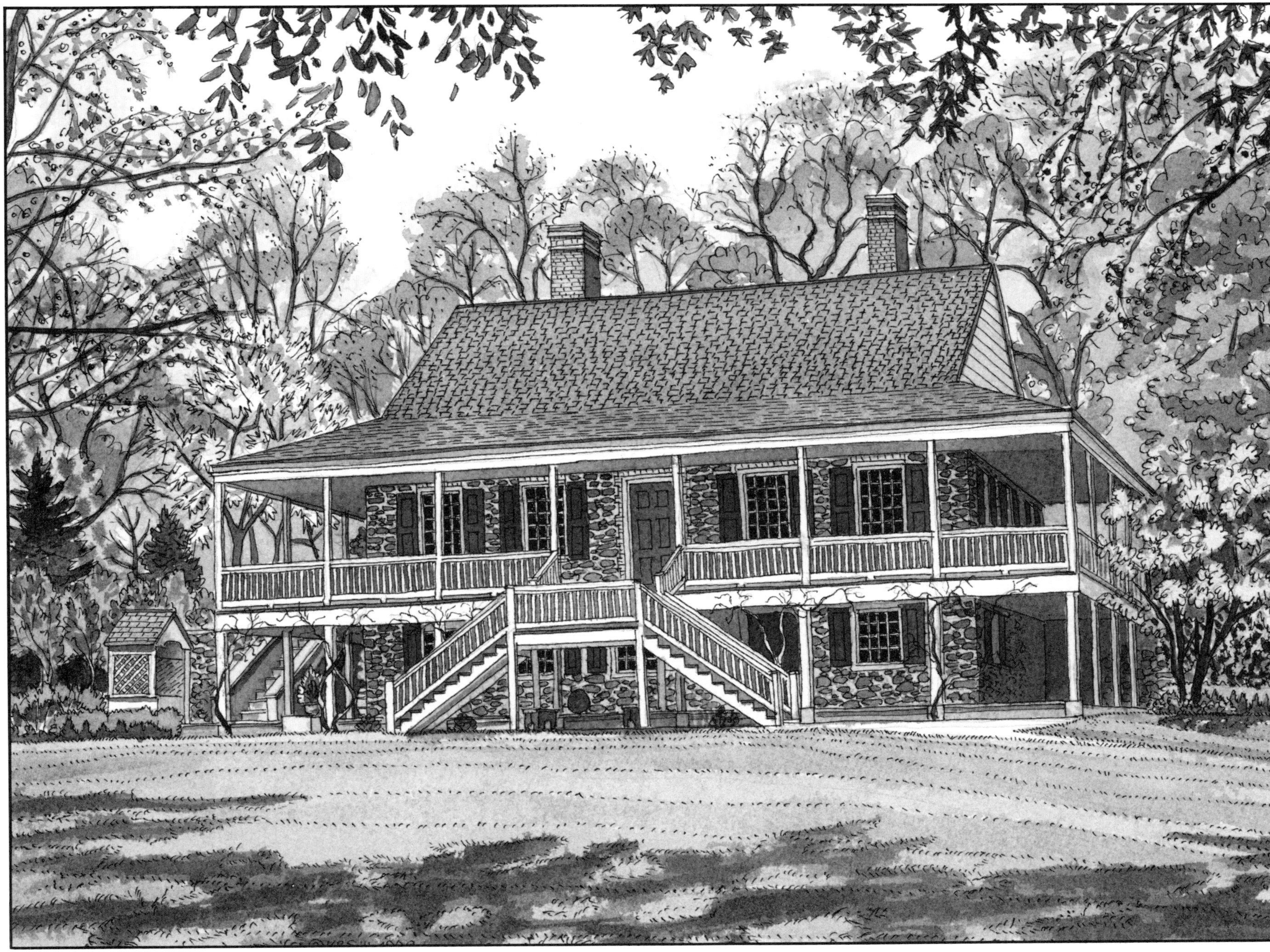

Knox Headquarters

Knox Headquarters is a Georgian stone house built in 1754 by Thomas Ellison, a successful miller and grain merchant, for his son John. An earlier wooden structure, built in 1734 to house the slaves who took care of Ellison's hunting dogs, became a wing of the new house. The house acquired its name during the Revolutionary War when Major General Henry Knox made it his headquarters for several important campaigns in the Hudson Valley. Generals Horatio Gates and Nathanael Greene also made the Ellison homestead their base of operations during the war.

Knox Headquarters remained in possession of Ellison descendants throughout most of the 19th century. It was purchsed by the Knox Headquarters Association in 1918 and transferred to New York State in 1922.

This Georgian home is more formal than many of the Dutch houses in the area with which it is contemporary and the stonework is softer and more rounded. The view is of the south facade. The wood building on the right side of the drawing may have been the original house.

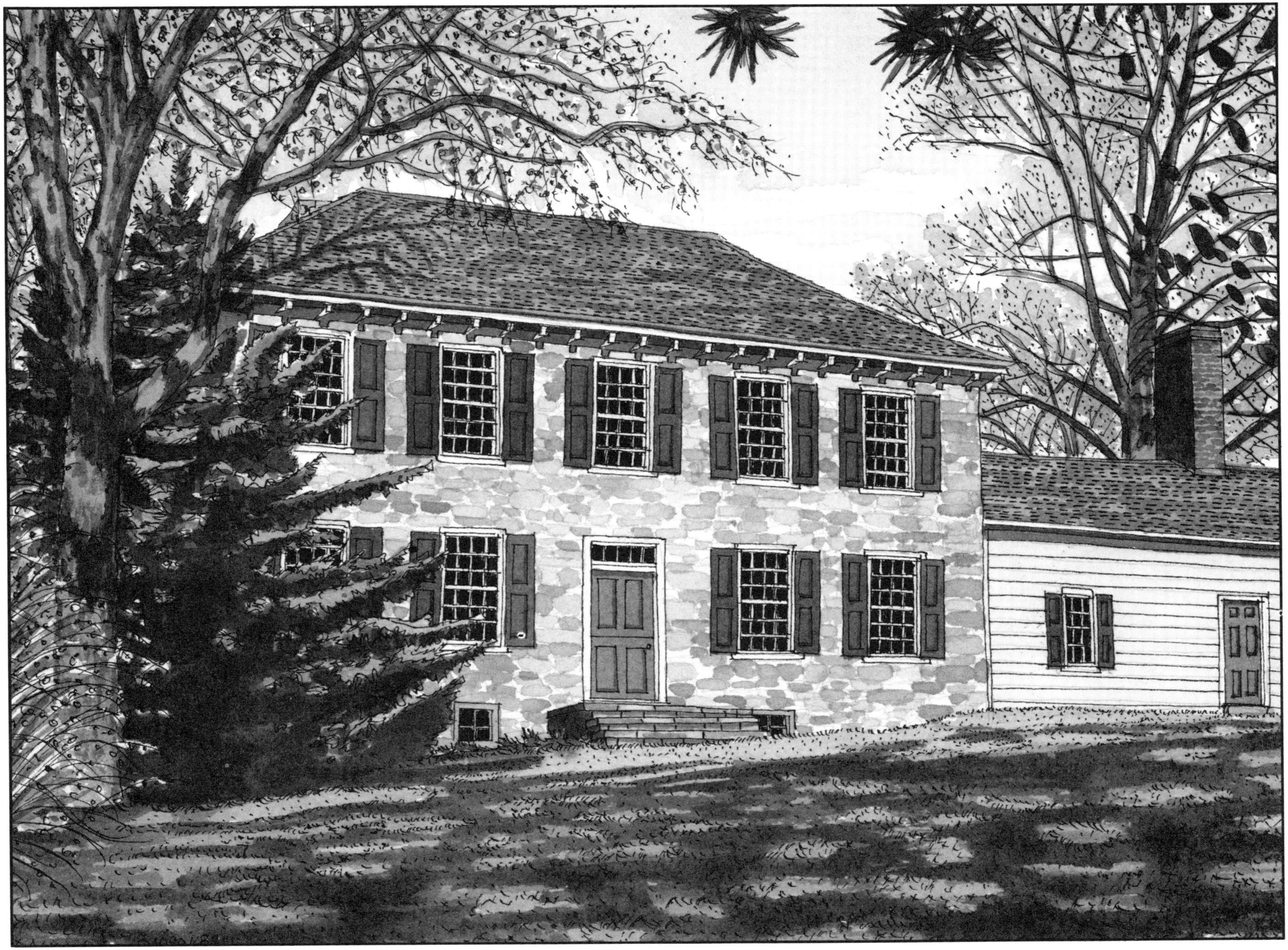

17 MANDEVILLE HOUSE

Jacob Mandeville, a New Yorker of Dutch descent, built Mandeville House in 1737. It was originally a one room Dutch-English farmhouse with an attic. Later, but still well before the Revolutionary War a kitchen wing and sitting rooms were added. During the Revolution the house, which was considered one of the finest in the area, stood along the road leading to the landing for ferries crossing between West Point and the east side of the Hudson. Because of its strategic location it served as headquarters for General Israel Putnam and was frequented by notables of the time, including Washington, Howe and Lafayette. Local historians like to point out that Washington's ledgers record payments to Mandeville House for rooms and services -- proof positive that he did, indeed, sleep here.

The prominent architect, Richard Upjohn, bought the house in 1852 and added the present library wing and Victorian Gothic touches to the design. In 1922 Mandeville House was bought by Colonel Julian Benjamin who stripped away Upjohn's Victorian overlay and restored the house to its earlier colonial style. Today it is owned and maintained by a private foundation.

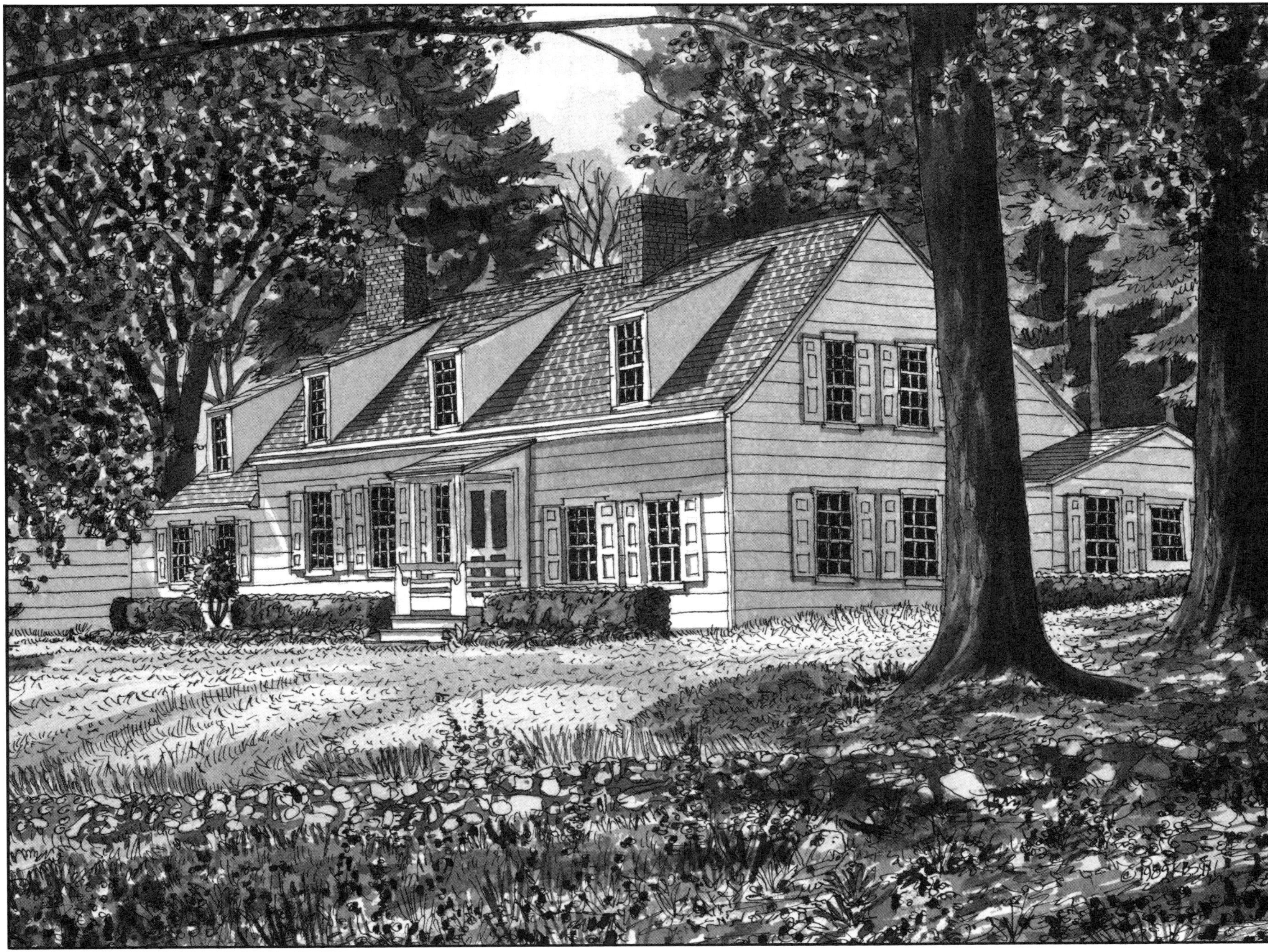

Schuyler Mansion

Philip John Schuyler was the son of a eminent early New York family who achieved prominence of his own as a businessman, landowner (he owned 125,000 acres in the upper Hudson area), delegate to the Continental Congress, major general in the Continental Army and, after the Revolution, one of New York State's first senators. In 1755 he married Catherine Van Rensselaer and in 1761 began planning this house which he designed and supervised through construction.

The mansion is a Georgian red brick structure with a double hipped roof and balustrade. It originally included wings at the rear that housed a nursery and offices, kitchen, smokehouse, garden shed, barn and coach house. They were demolished in the mid 19th century but their foundations have been excavated and flower beds planted to mark their locations.

Schuyler Mansion was host to many important guests in its day: George Washington, Benjamin Franklin and Benedict Arnold among them. The marriage of Schuyler's daughter, Elizabeth, to Alexander Hamilton took place in the drawing room in 1780. The Mansion passed out of family hands in 1804 and had a succession of owners until it was acquired by the state in 1912.

Drawing Schuyler Mansion was a challenge. The house, which was once called "The Pastures", is now encircled by the city of Albany. The east facade shown here presented the only good angle on the building but is poised high above street level with a wall and thick growth of trees in front. I wcrked on the sidewalk below and across the street, looking through the trees and piecing together the view.

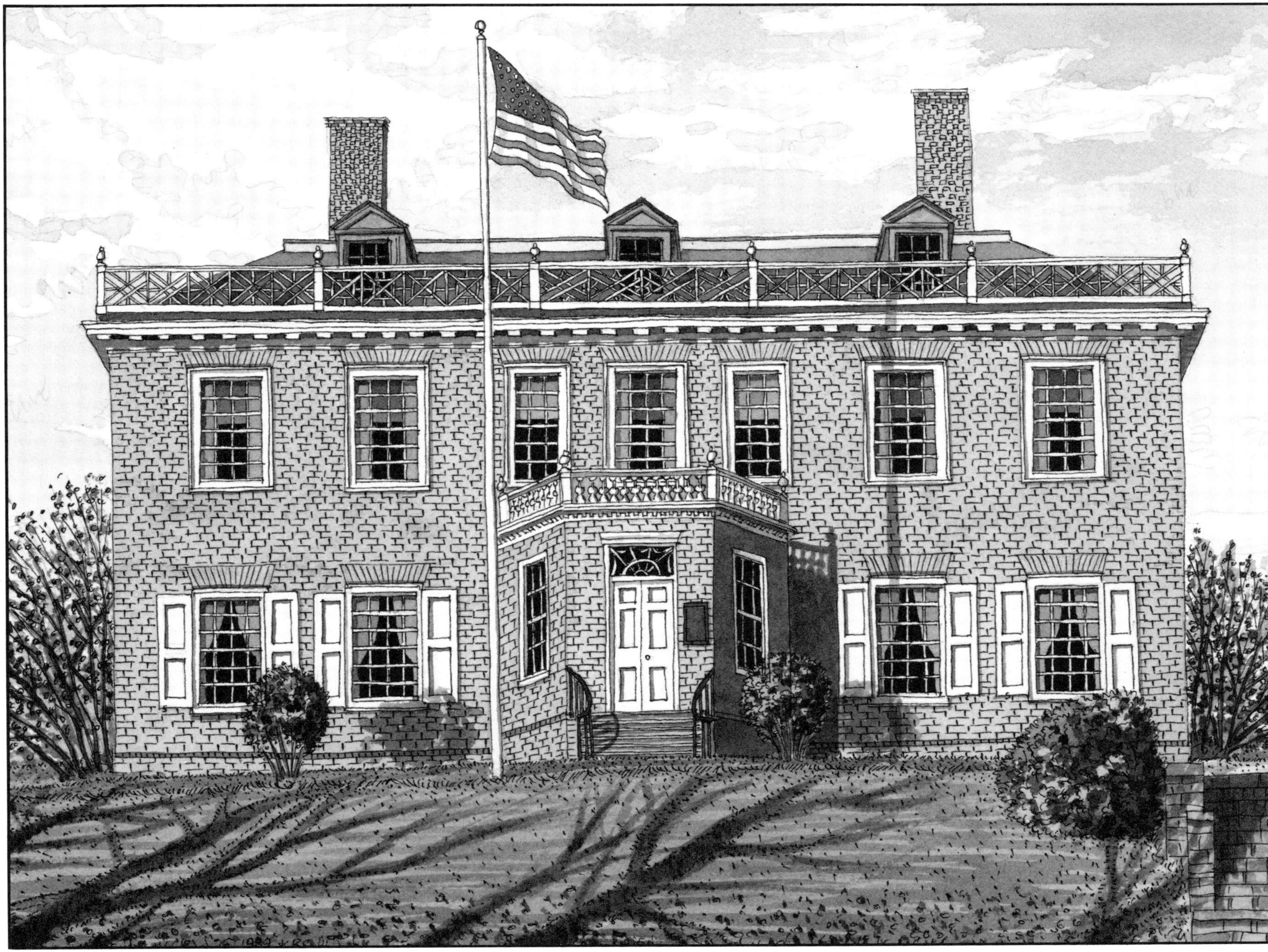

New Windsor Cantonment

This simple log cabin is the only known existing structure built by revolutionary soldiers. The New Windsor Cantonment in which it is located was the winter home for between six and eight thousand Continental troops during the final year of the war while the peace treaty was being negotiated in Paris.

The Cantonment held about seven hundred military buildings, including many huts like this one, each built by the sixteen soldiers who were to inhabit it. When the peace treaty was announced in 1783, the weary, underpaid army dispersed and the buildings in the Cantonment were auctioned, dismantled and carried away. One hut, acquired by a man named Sackett, was carted a few miles from the encampment and rebuilt as part of his house. The clapboard siding and metal roof with which he clad the structure protected it for a century and a half until 1934, when it was returned to the Cantonment and restored.

I chose to draw this simple cabin because it is the most basic example of early building -- a starting point. Its hand-hewn, rough, utilitarian structure is generic American in style. This view of the southwest facade shows the cabin's weathered wood chinked with a plaster-like material and its split cedar-shaked roof.

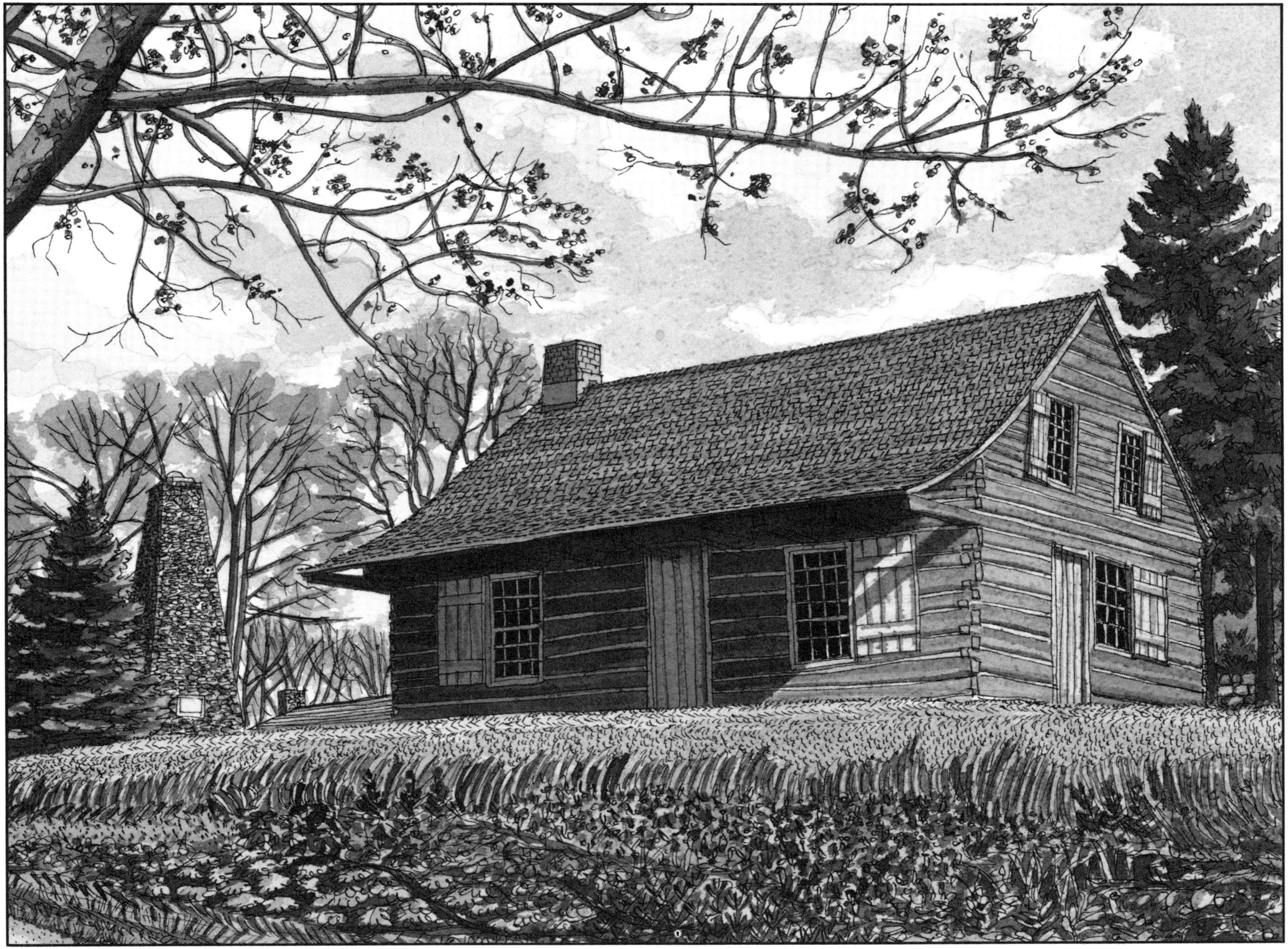

CLINTON HOUSE

Clinton House is a stone structure built in 1765 and rebuilt, after a fire, in 1783. It served as an official headquarters during 1777 when the new state government was located in Poughkeepsie. Today it is the home of the Dutchess County Historical Society and has a library of more than 10,000 books and documents dating from the 18th century.

I decided to draw Clinton House after talking to a curator at the Dutchess County Historical Society who convinced me of the importance of small, modest buildings such as this one which do not receive the same attention paid the great estates on the river but are, nevertheless, important historical treasures. It is in this building that the documentation for historic buildings throughout Dutchess County is carried out. Today Clinton House is in an entirely urban setting.

I left the chain link fence, the cars and the neighborhood children out of this drawing of the building's south facade.

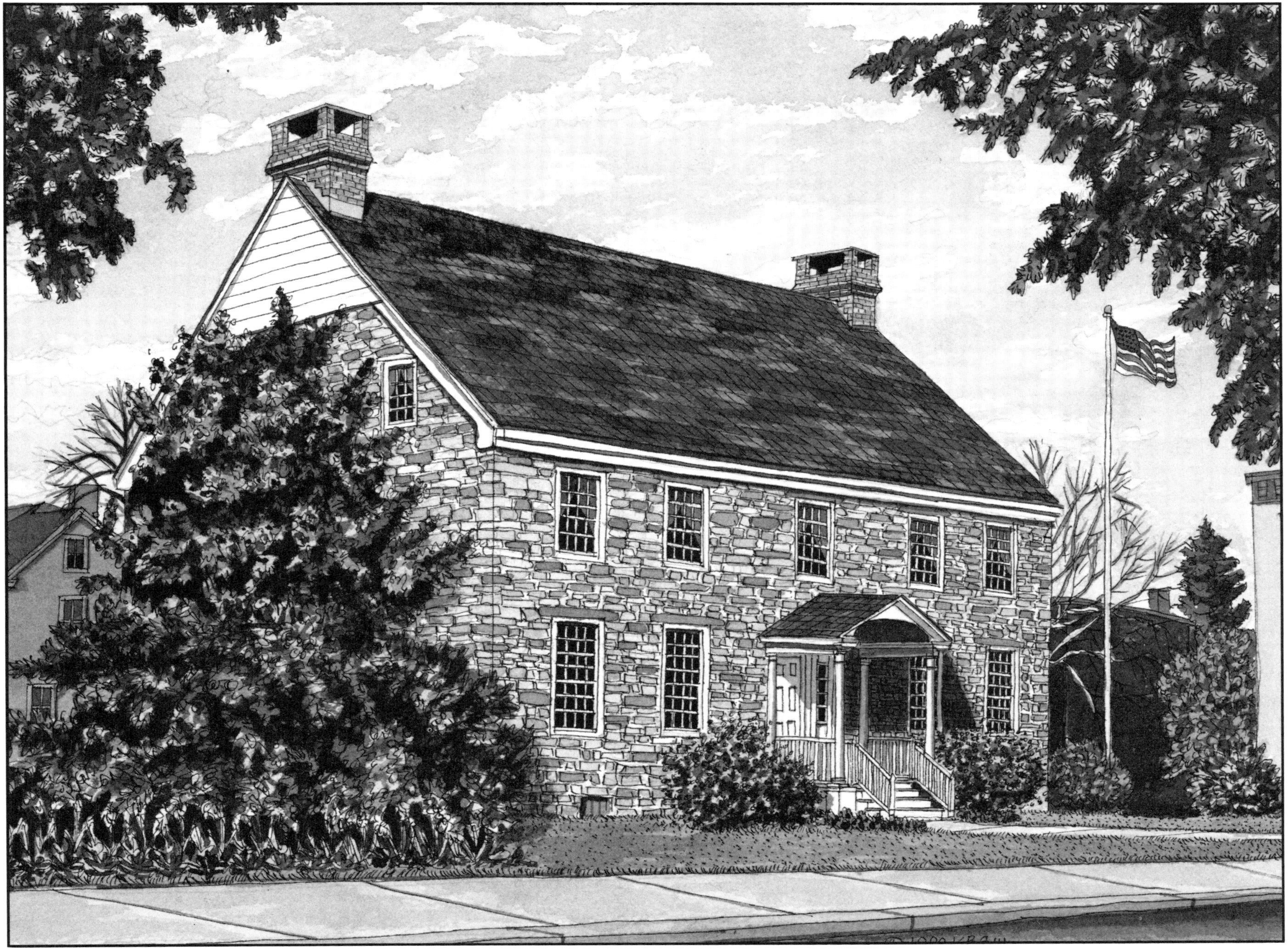

Senate House

The stone house in Kingston where the first New York State Senate met is known as Senate House. It was built in the early 18th century by Wessel Ten Broeck on a site overlooking Esopus Creek. The exact construction of the original house is not known, as it was partially destroyed by fire in 1777, but historians believe it consisted of a simple central hall with a staircase flanked by rooms on either side and a separate kitchen. Abraham Gaasbeek, who acquired the house in 1751, is believed to have rebuilt the main section of the house sometime before his death in 1794.

The location of the house in Kingston placed it at the center of political activity during the Revolution. It was in that city that the New York State Constitution was adopted; George Clinton, the first governor, was sworn into office; and the first State Senate met on September 9, 1777. Kingston was, for a time, the de facto capital of the state.

During the 19th century, wooden additions were made to the building. After its purchase by New York State in 1887 they were removed and a stone porch and kitchen wing were added. Changes in dormers, roof and windows have been made over the years as more accurate information about the architecture of the period is gained.

This view of the east facade shows an unprepossessing building that slowly reveals its character. As I sat and sketched I was aware of a palpable sense of history -- the feeling of people coming and going through its doors.

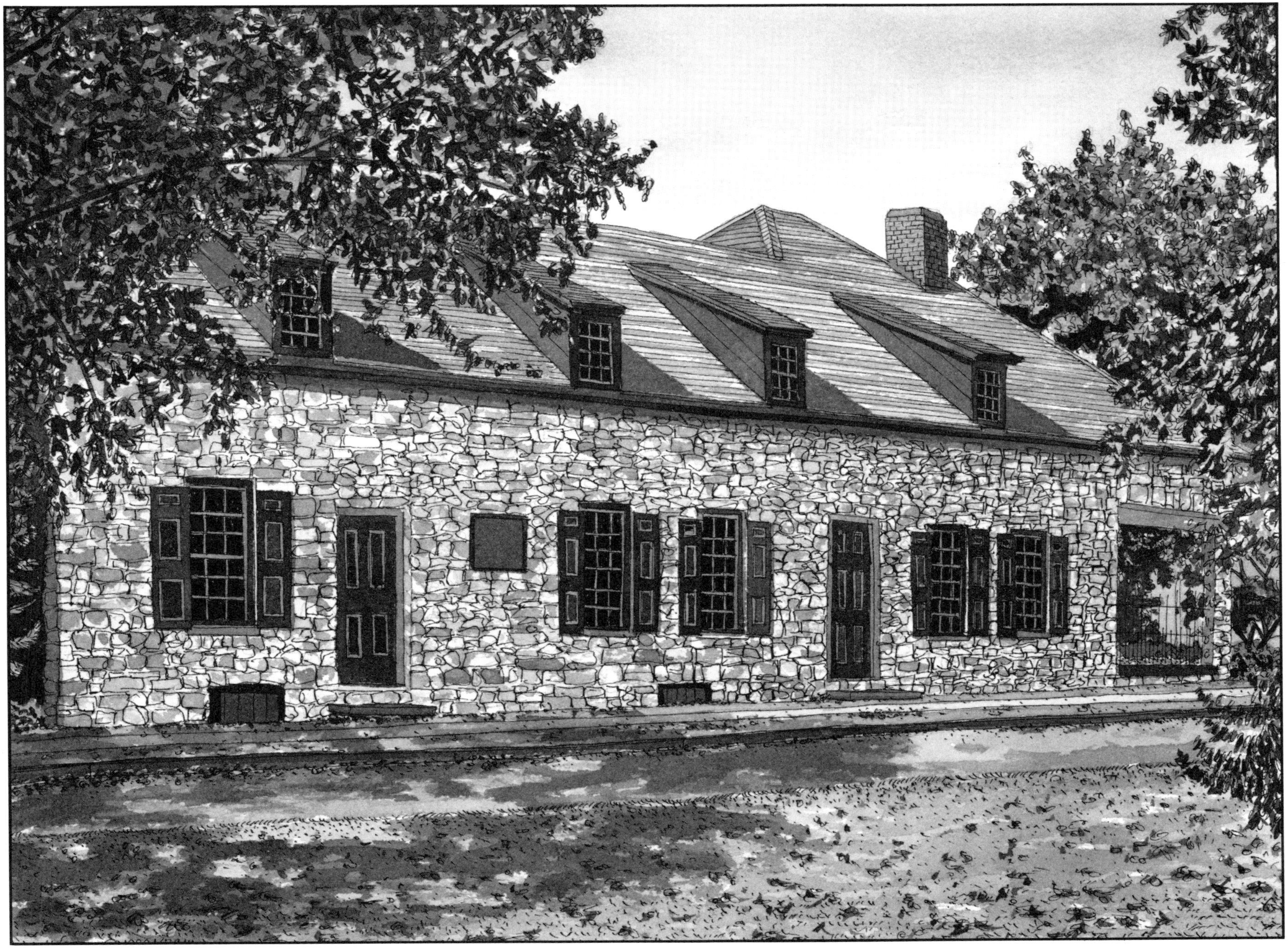

DePuy Canal House

This stone inn was built for Simon DePuy in 1797. The Delaware and Hudson Canal, which opened in 1828, passed within yards of the building and, until its demise in 1899, made the Canal House a prosperous, flourishing hostelry. A restored lock now stands not far from the tavern as a reminder of times when the highways of American commerce were its rivers. Today the inn is restored and is operated as a fine restaurant.

The Canal House appeals to me because it speaks to the era of canals and westward expansion. It is a good example of a large stone building and is, in fact, bigger than many of the other Dutch stone buildings in the region. In this view of the east facade of the building I hoped to convey its comfortable, welcoming feeling.

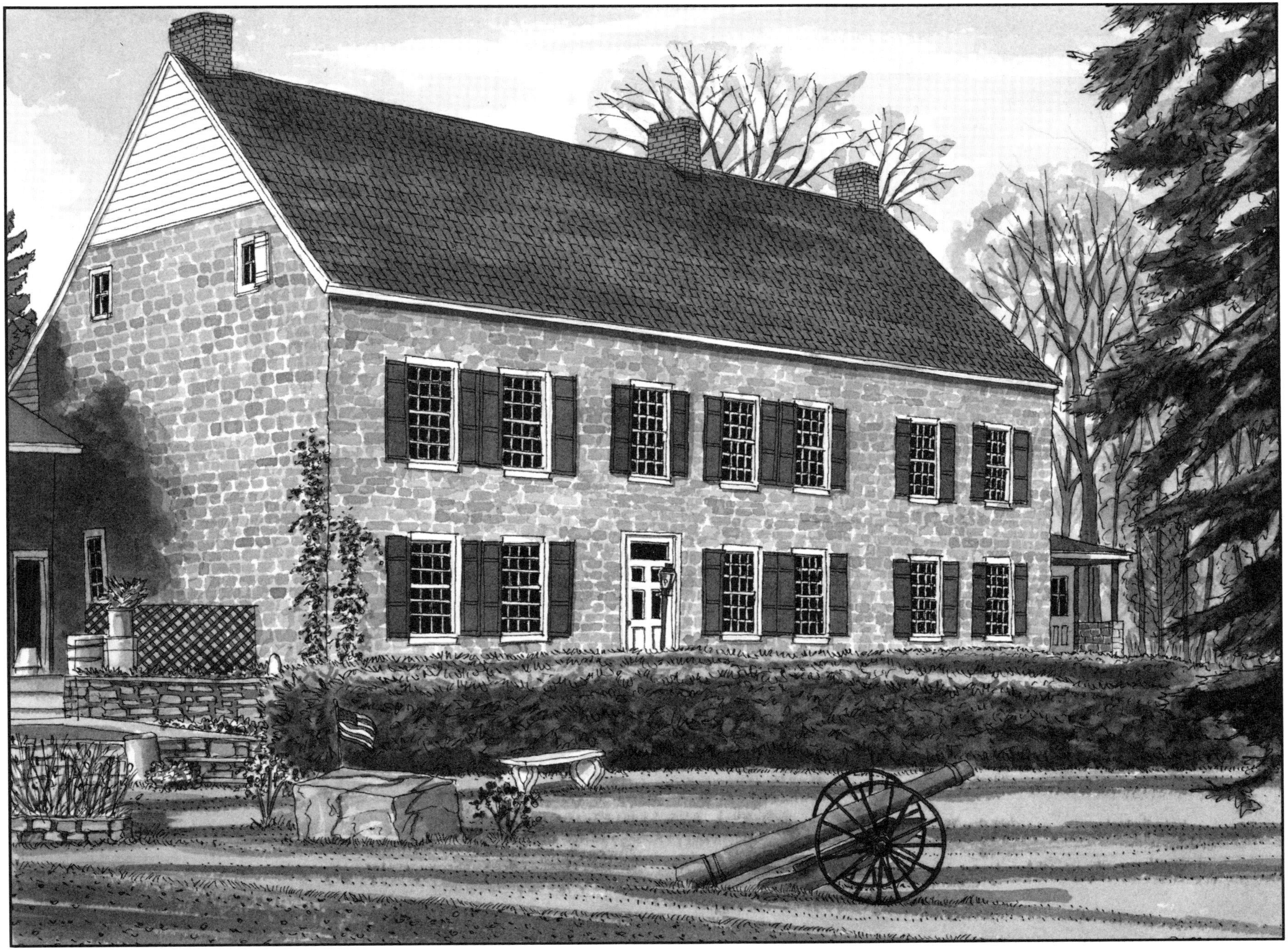

23 LINDENWALD

In 1839 Martin Van Buren, the eighth president of the United States, purchased Lindenwald, a Federal style mansion built by Peter Van Ness. It was intended as a retirement home and Van Buren lived here until his death in 1862. In 1848 his youngest son retained Richard Upjohn, architect of Trinity Church in New York City, to re-design the building in the style of an Italian villa. Upjohn created a thirty-six room mansion with a four storey brick tower.

The house passed out of family hands and had several owners until it was purchased by the federal government in 1974. It has since been restored to appear as it was during President Van Buren's lifetime and is operated by the National Park Service.

Lindenwald is sited on a beautiful, open property dotted with very large pines. Its architectural history is writ large in its combination of Federal structure, Italianate tower and Victorian details. I made this drawing of the east facade on a bright, clear October day when the sun, reflecting on the pale yellow paint of the house, provided striking contrasts of light and shadow.

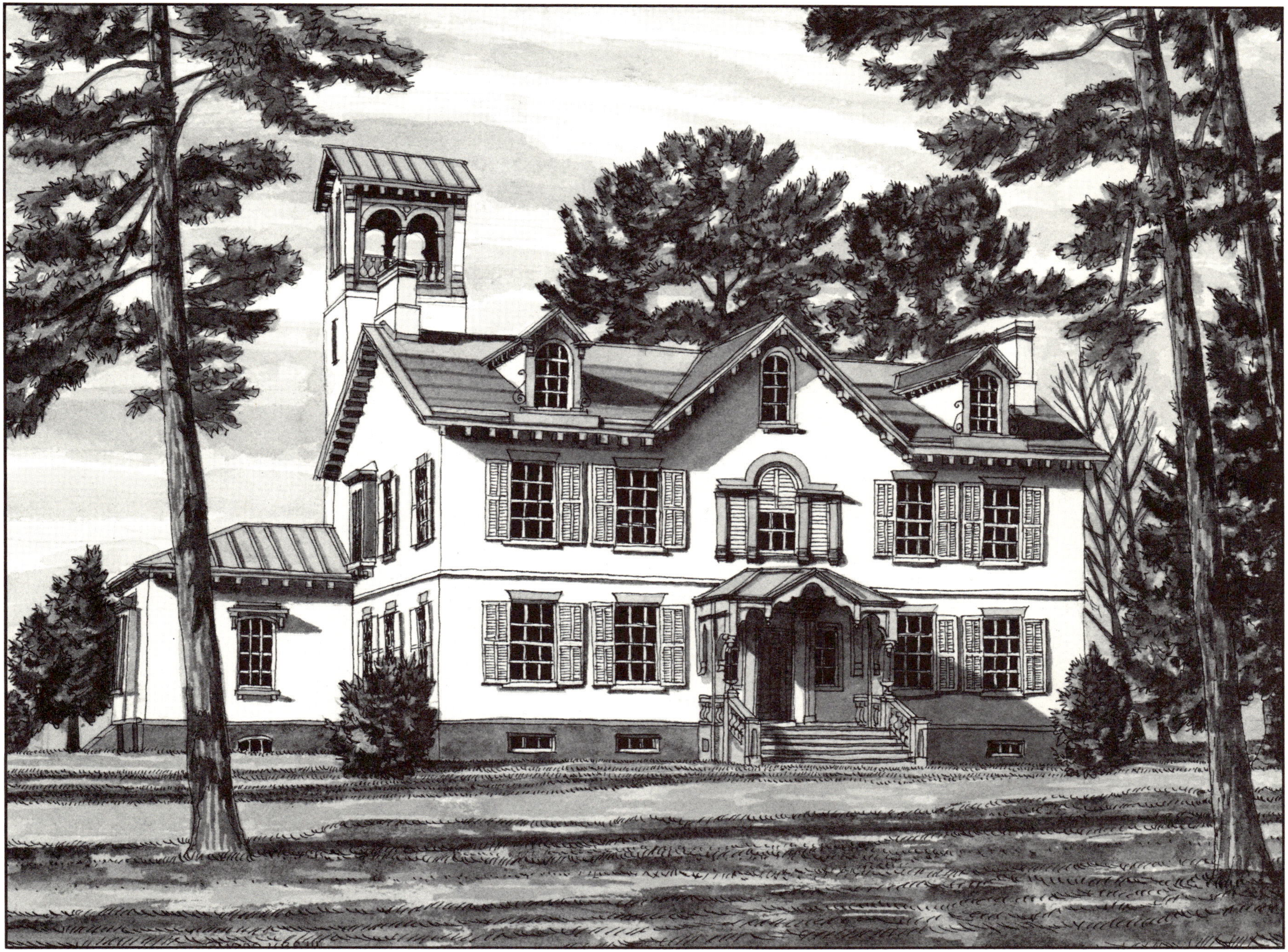

Ten Broeck House

The first Ten Broeck to arrive in the new world came with Peter Minuit in the early 17th century. Abraham Ten Broeck, a descendant of that early settler and the builder of this house overlooking the Hudson at Albany, was mayor of that city, a general in the Continental Army and a member of the State Senate. He built the house, which was designed by architect Phillip Hooker, in 1798.

Ten Broeck House is Federal in style, although the interior has a Georgian plan. Renovations in the mid 19th century altered the architect's original layout. The house was purchased by Theodore Olcott in 1848 and members of the Olcott family lived in it until 1947 when it was donated to the Albany County Historical Society.

The plain brick facade, with its little Ionic porch, gives Ten Broeck an austere bearing. But it is a good example of a solidly built, upright house for the well-to-do 19th century family. The drawing depicts the east facade.

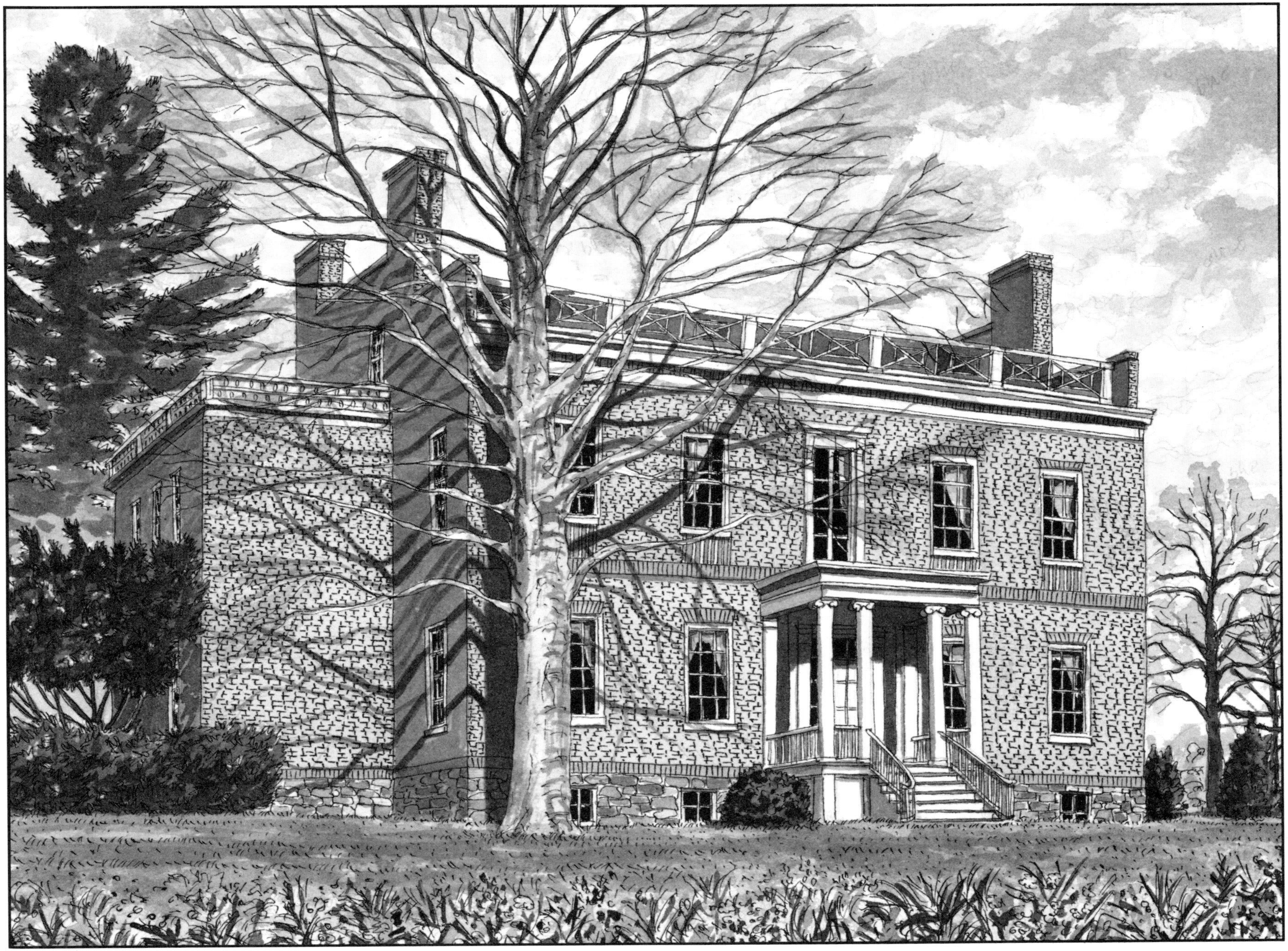

Montgomery Place

Janet Livingston Montgomery built Chateau de Montgomery, a two storey, five bay Federal mansion, in 1805. It soon gained repute as one of the finest manor houses in America and, thanks to Janet's interest in gardening and landscaping, one of the most beautiful properties as well. In the early 1840's Livingston descendants commissioned Alexander Jackson Davis to carry out extensive additions and alterations to the estate. The architect added a north pavilion, west veranda, symmetrical semi-octagonal south wing and several smaller detached structures to the property. Davis was again retained in 1863 and this time added an east portico, a terrace and a roof balustrade.

During the second quarter of the 20th century Montgomery Place was inhabited by Livingston descendant General Ross Delafield and his wife Violetta White. Violetta expanded the plantings on the vast property and re-designed portions of the landscaping to include formal herb and rose gardens and a rustic 'rough garden' of rocks and ferns. Today the 434 acre estate includes over 150 acres of fruit bearing trees. Montgomery Place was acquired by Historic Hudson Valley in 1986 and is now undergoing extensive restoration.

Montgomery Place is one of the more ornate Federal style buildings in the valley. It is characterised by an abundance of applied detail including swags and elaborate moldings. I have drawn the east facade of the house. It is interesting to note that the stone texture shown in the drawing is a faux finish of applied sand over the wood exterior of the structure.

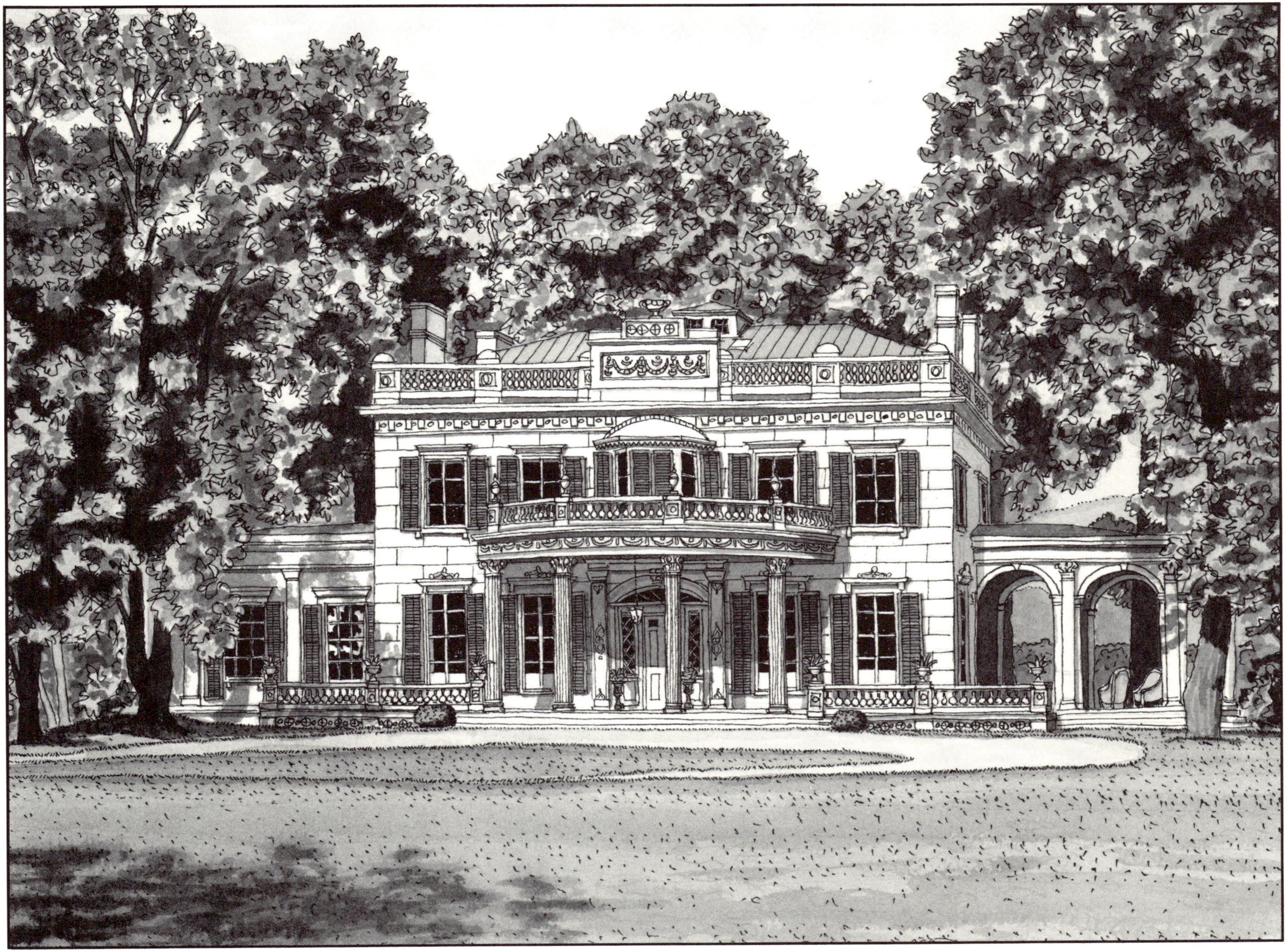

BOSCOBEL

Boscobel was built between 1804 and 1808 by States Morris Dyckman, a loyalist who returned to England after the Revolutionary War and brought back with him the plans for this Adam style mansion, a style that was in vogue in England at the time. The house was originally located in Montrose and was inhabited by descendants of the Dyckman family until the late 19th century.

Boscobel had several owners in the following decades, and in 1924 was acquired by Westchester County as a park. The grand house was twice threatened with demolition and in 1955 was dismantled and stored while funding for its restoration and a new site were sought. Thanks largely to a substantial grant from Lila Acheson Wallace the house was rebuilt in 1957 on its current site overlooking the Hudson River in Garrison. The interior has been completely restored and furnished with an extraordinary collection of Federal pieces.

I have drawn the southwest facade of what is to me one of the loveliest houses on the river. The building is elegant, the gardens beautifully laid out and tended and the views down the river among the longest of any house in the valley. Boscobel's many large windows open it to the river and the surrounding countryside and fill the inside with light. This view shows the smooth board construction on the river side of the house (in contrast to clapboard construction on the other sides) and the unusual carved wooden draperies on the second floor balcony.

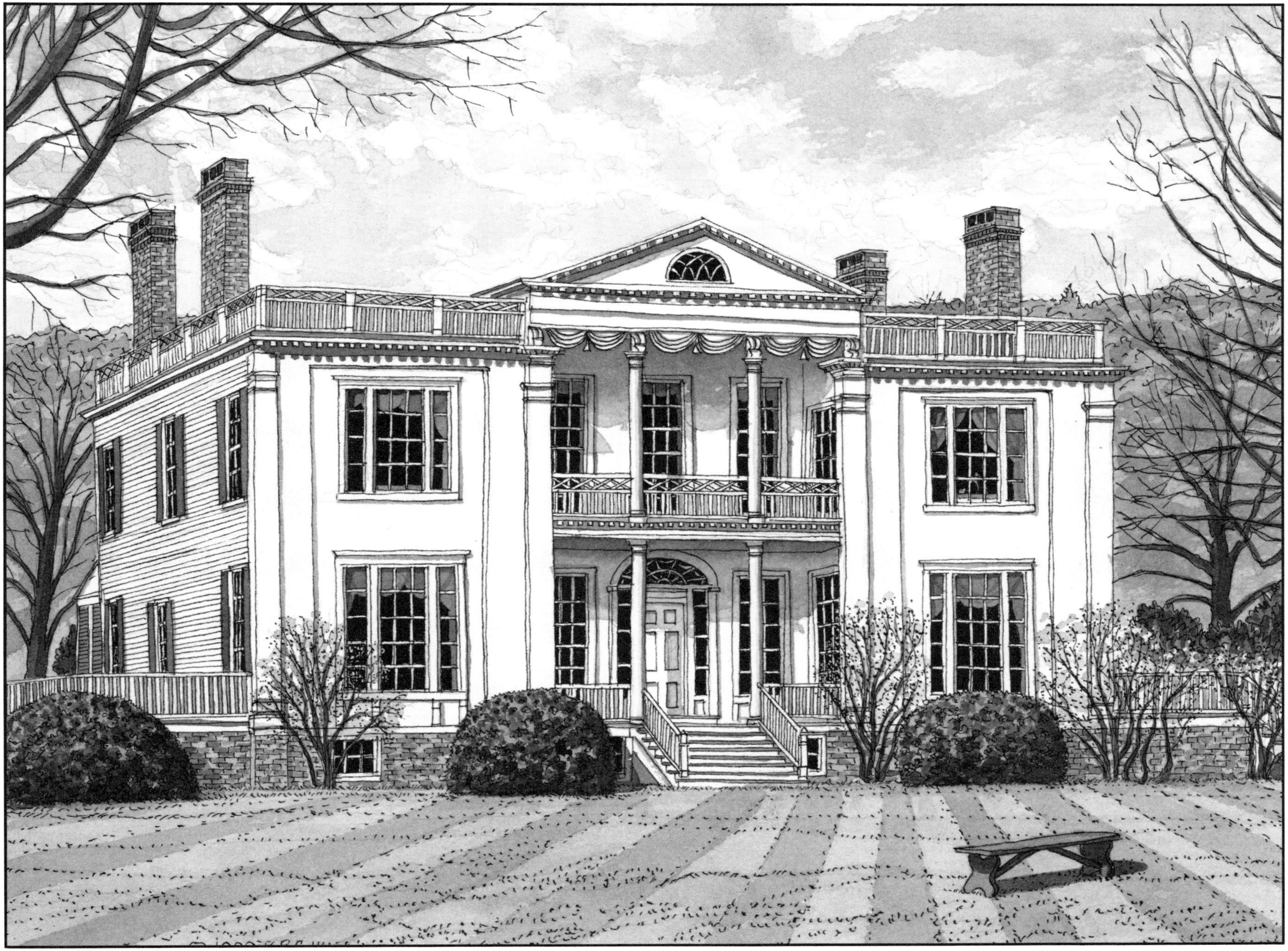

ROKEBY

In 1814 John Armstrong and his wife Alida Livingston built a two-storey, twenty room stone house on land that was part of the vast Beekman/Livingston patent. They called it La Bergerie, or 'the sheepfold', after a gift of Merino sheep given to Armstrong by Napoleon on the occasion of Armstrong's departure from France as a former Minister to the French Court.

The Armstrong's daughter Margaret and her husband, a son of John Jacob Astor, took possession of the house in 1836 and renamed it Rokeby after a poem by Sir Walter Scott. They enlarged the house, more than doubling its size. The Astor's improvements included a Gothic Revival library built within a many-sided tower wing and the re-design of the gardens by European landscape architect Hans Ludwig Ehlers.

Generations of Astors have occupied the house to the present day, including the ten orphaned children of Margaret Astor Ward and John Winthrop Chanler, heirs to the Astor fortune who were raised at Rokeby by guardians. At the turn of the century two important figures in the history of Amerian architecture and landscape design left their marks on Rokeby. Architect Stanford White remodeled the house and the Olmsted brothers redesigned the gardens.

Today Rokeby is owned by descendants of the Astor family who are active in the effort to have it, and other grand estates in the Hudson River Valley, protected and restored as national historic treasures.

On my visit to Rokeby I was greeted by Winthrop Aldrich, one of the present owners of the property who has lived with his family in part of the mansion. Rokeby is alive with memories. Faint remains of fresco-like paintings on the front wall of the house recall the family mythology of the Merino sheep. My drawing of the south facade shows the building's stuccoed fieldstone exterior and the curious blend of Italian influences and mansard roof. The house commands some of the finest views of the Catskill Mountains to be had from the east side of the river.

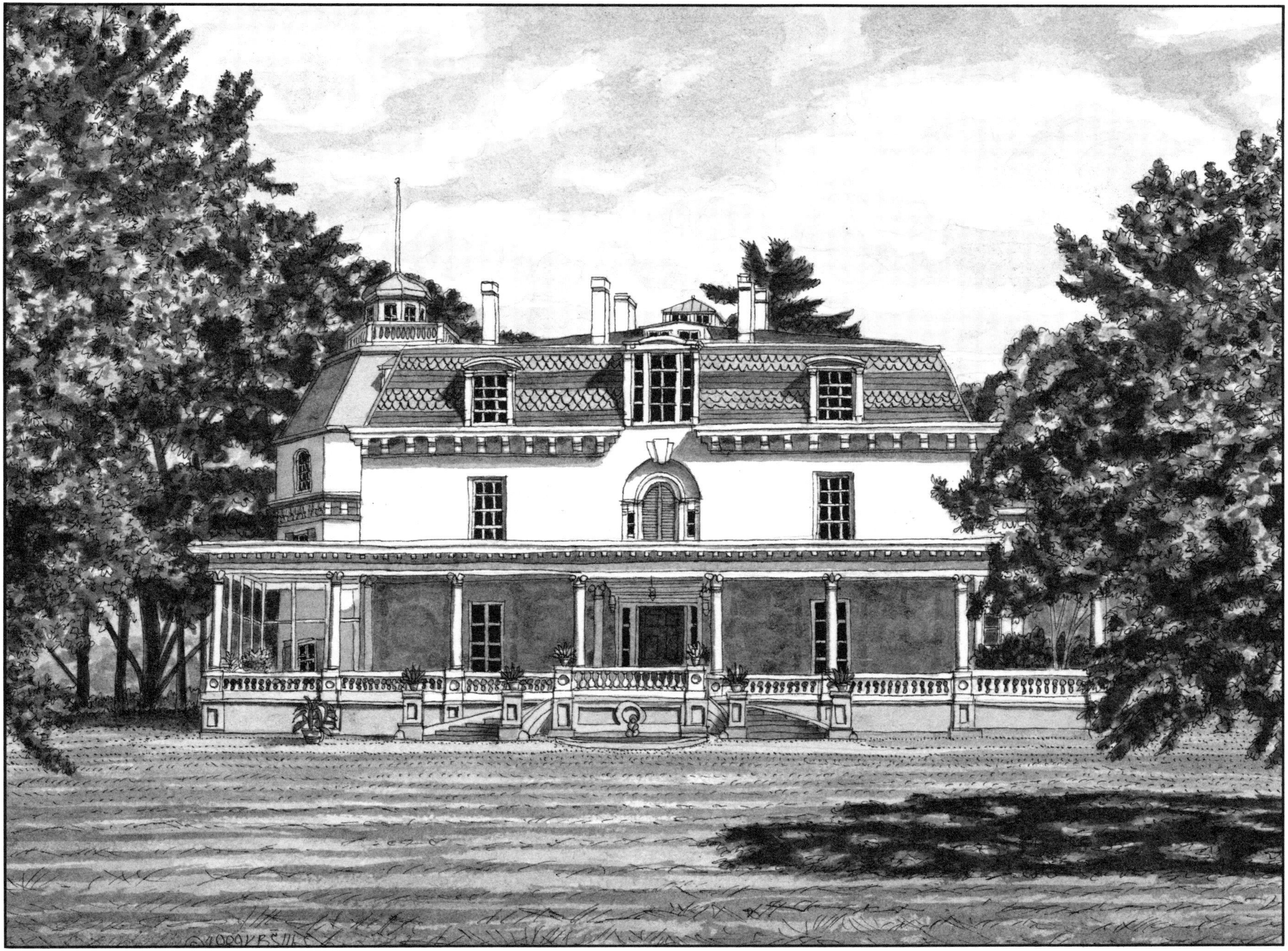

Putnam County Court House

Built in 1814, this Greek Revival wood building is the oldest court house in continuous service in New York State. It is located in Carmel, the Putnam County seat, on the shore of Lake Gleneida. The court house and jail, which is attached to the back of the building, were built by contractor John Townsend for the sum of $3382.86. Fire destroyed the second storey and roof of the building in 1924, but they were reconstructed with the support of a concerned citizenry.

I think it appropriate that this very simple version of a Greek temple should fulfill a judicial function. The year in which it was built marked the beginning of the Greek Revival movement in this country -- a movement grounded in a strong feeling of identity between the aims of the new democracy and the values of ancient Greece. This simple building was an embodiment of noble hopes and dreams for the new republic. Funding is now being sought to underwrite the costs of a newly-begun restoration program.

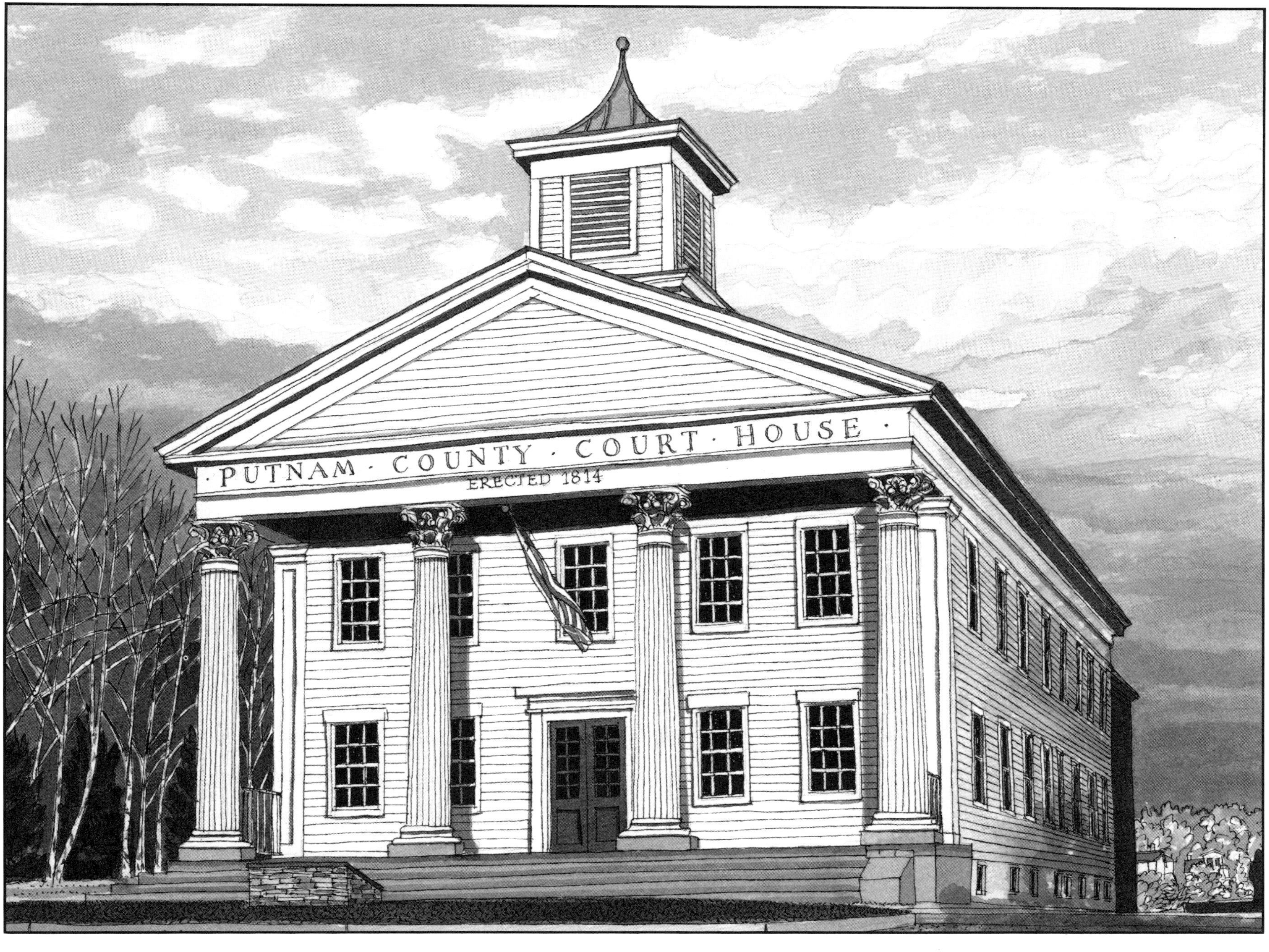
· PUTNAM · COUNTY · COURT · HOUSE ·
ERECTED 1814

CEDAR GROVE

Cedar Grove is a Federal style brick house built in 1816 for the Barton family of Greene County. Thomas Cole, originator of the Hudson River school of painting and inspirer of a national tradition of landscape painting, married Maria Barton in 1836 and established residency here. Cole lived and worked on the site from 1836 to 1848. In 1846 he built a large Italianate studio that has, regrettably, been destroyed. In Cole's time the house enjoyed panoramic views of the Catskills. They are familiar views to anyone who knows his canvasses. The house is now a National Historic Landmark.

Cedar Grove is somewhat surprising in its modesty when compared to the grand paintings of the man who lived here, but the character of the man explains the disparity. Thomas Cole was a modest man whose primary concern was his work. He wanted to be comfortable but did not share the desire for opulence or the interest in exploring architecture on a grand scale that motivated other artists such as Church and Morse. The drawing depicts the south facade of the small house that, although set on a hill, is now surrounded by an expanding neighborhood. The views that Thomas Cole saw from Cedar Grove now live only in the paintings.

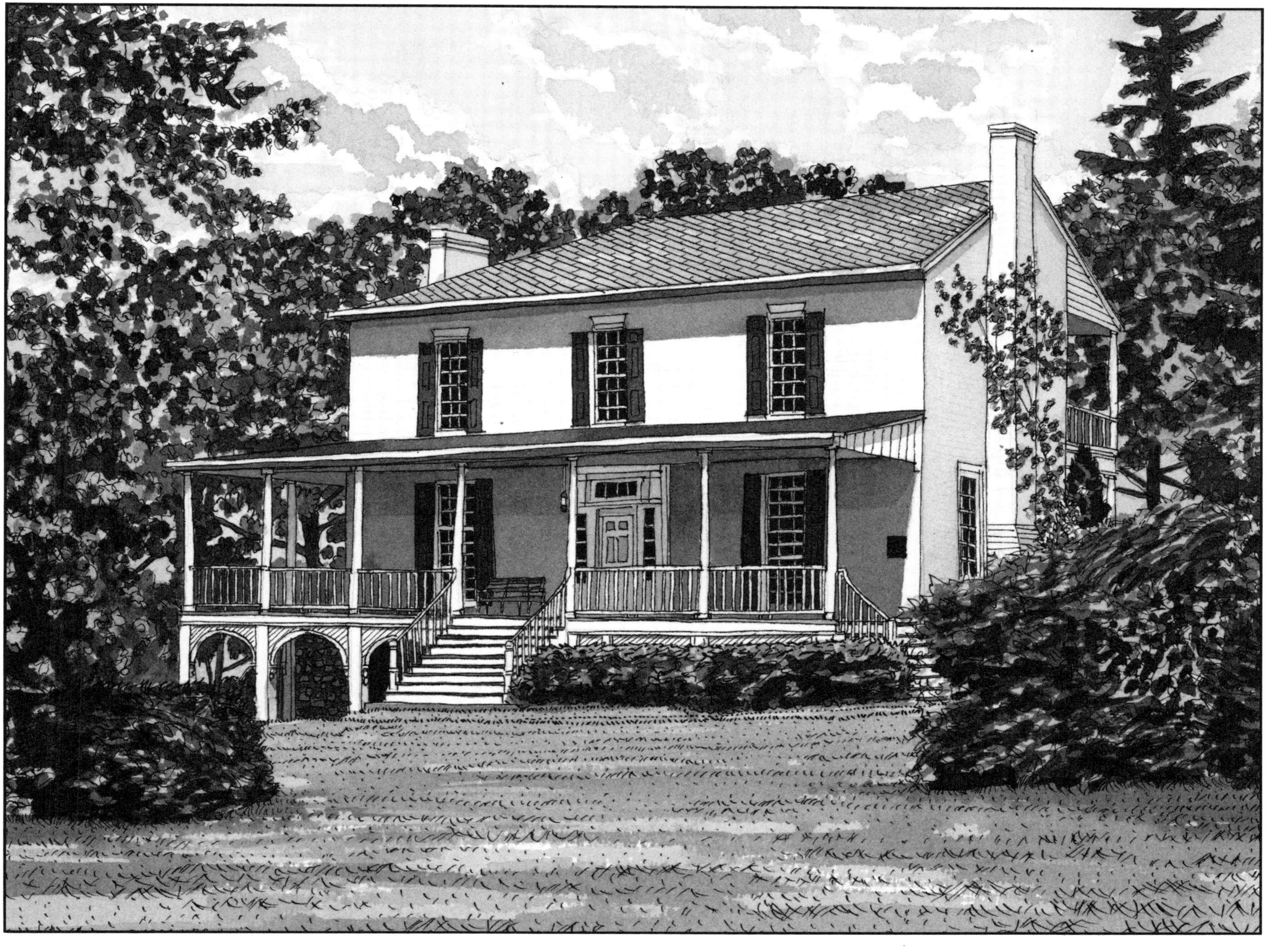

VANDERPOEL HOUSE

James Vanderpoel was a lawyer and judge who was active in the politics and public life of early 19th century Kingston and Albany. In 1819 he commissioned builder Barnabus Waterman to construct a gracious Federal style home, based on plans published in builder's guides of the time. The house combines Hudson Valley architectural traditions with a New England style influenced by the classicism of Robert Adam. It is characterized by delicate ornament, high ceilings and generously proportioned windows and is furnished with fine pieces by New York cabinetmakers.

Vanderpoel House is an elegantly proportioned house of rosy colored brick. It boasts especially fine fan and side lights on its central bay. The east and west facades of the house are mirror images. I drew the east facade to take advantage of the morning light.

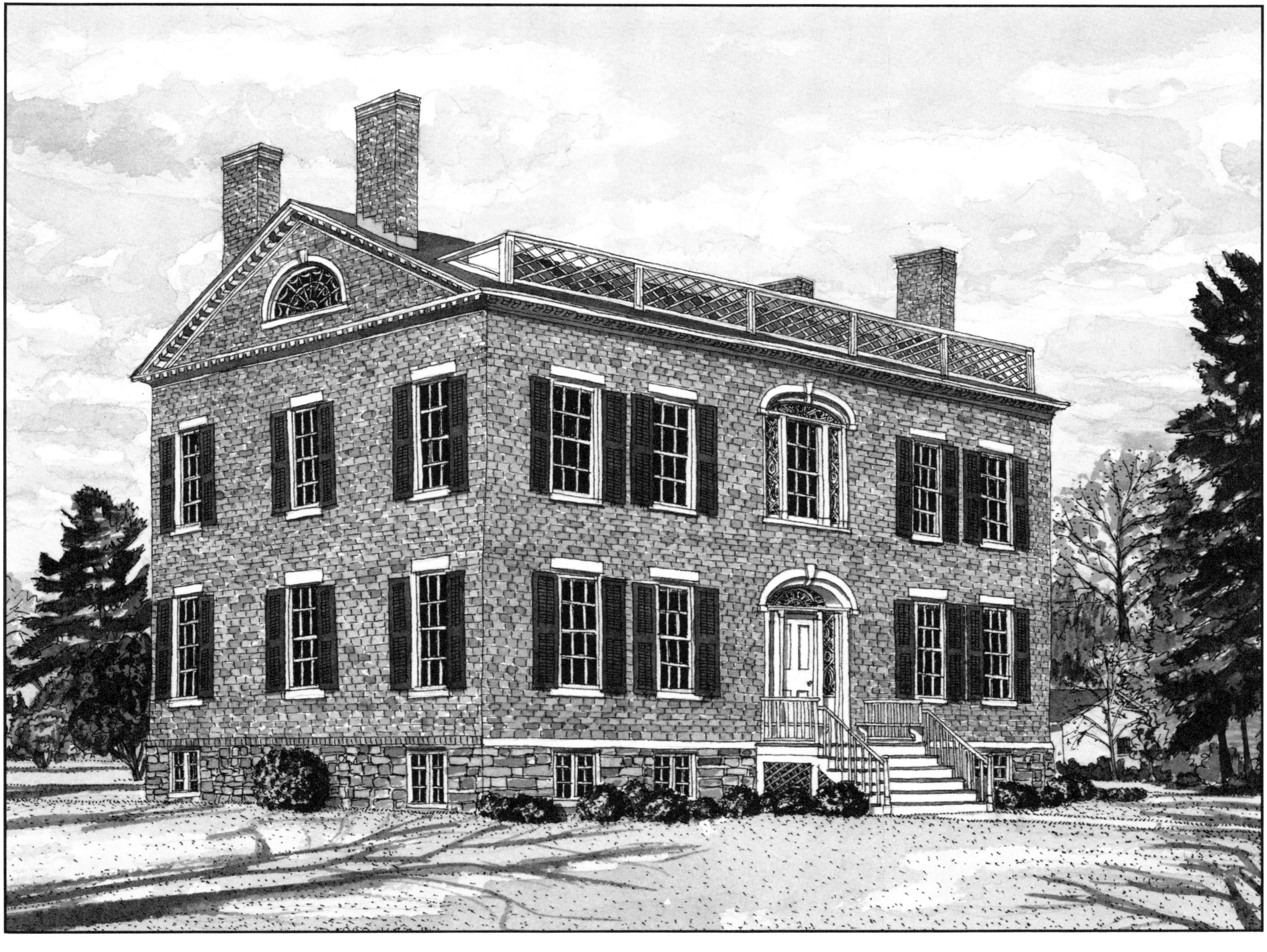

31 EDGEWATER

Edgewater was built in 1821 by John Livingston for his daughter Margaretta and her husband, Captain Lowndes Brown. The name of the property reflects its siting right at the river's edge. (Today it is sandwiched between the railroad and the river.) Its design is generally attributed to the neo-classic revivalist architect, Robert Mills. In 1852 Margaretta sold the house to Robert Donaldson, owner of Blithewood, who retained architect Alexander Jackson Davis to enlarge it. Davis' additions include an octagonal library on the north side of the house and a conservatory annexed to the dining room.

In the 20th century, Edgewater has had several owners, among them the writer Gore Vidal who made it his home for twenty years, and financier Richard Jenrette who purchased the property in 1969 and has restored it to its neo-classic grandeur and furnished it using Donaldson's 1872 inventory.

Edgewater is a brick and stucco structure with columns faux-finished to look like cut stone. The contemporary artist Robert Jackson has done extensive faux finishing, stenciling and marbleizing in the interior. The drawing depicts the west facade of the building which overlooks the river and its many small coves and lovely tree-shaded points.

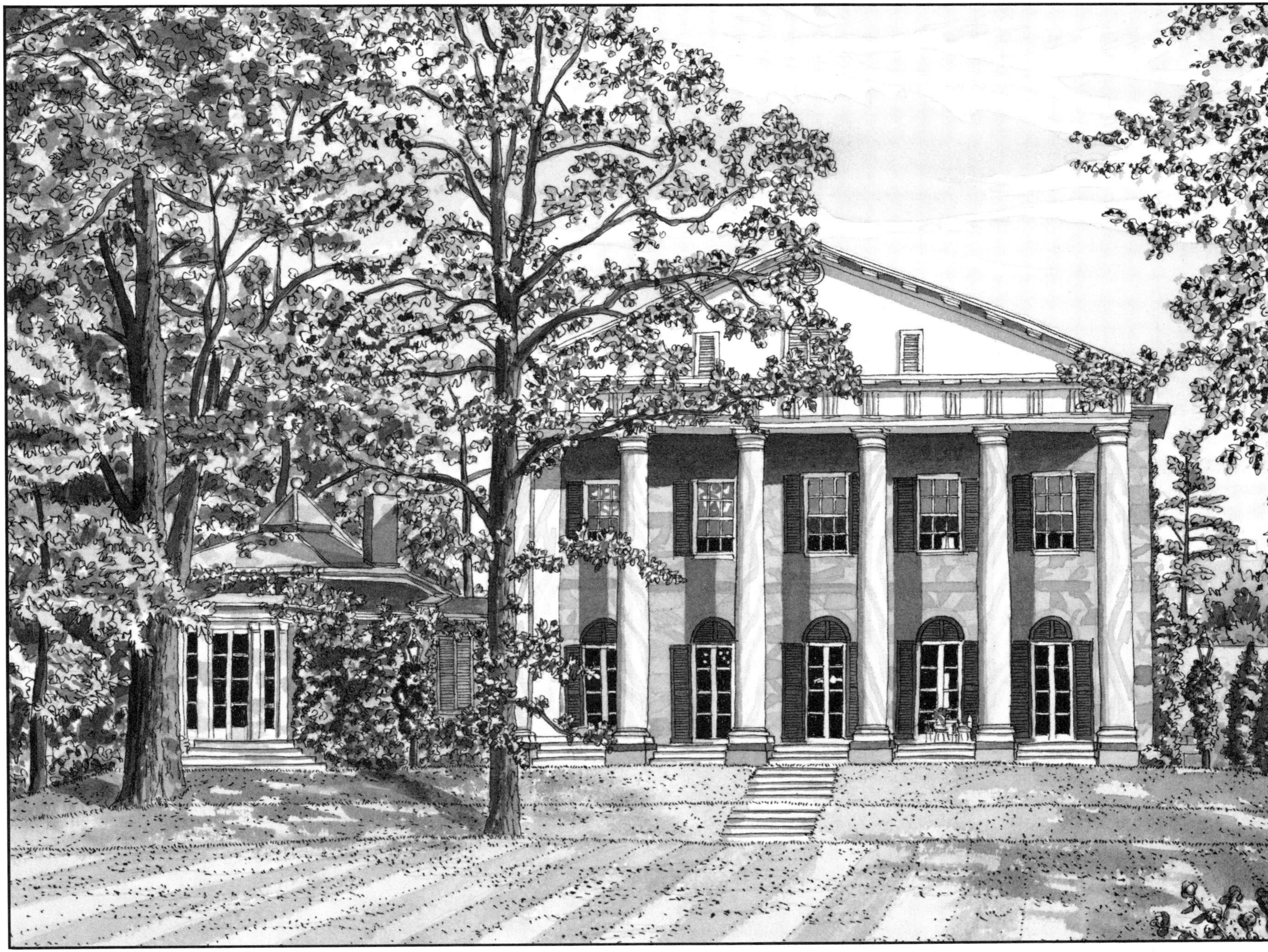

SPRINGWOOD

Franklin Delano Roosevelt was born at Springwood, and he and his wife, Eleanor, are buried in the rose garden. It was his beloved childhood home, his election night retreat and the summer White House during the years of his presidency. His father, James Roosevelt, bought the early 19th century clapboard and wood-frame house in 1867 and, over the following two decades, enlarged and remodeled it in the style of an Italian villa.

In 1915 the widowed Sara Roosevelt commissioned prominent architects Hoppin & Koen to re-design the villa. Their work defined the buiding as it stands today: a thirty-five room Georgian Revival Mansion.

Roosevelt had strong ties to the Hudson Valley. His family had maintained a home in the region for four generations. Shortly before his death he donated a piece of land at Hyde Park to the United States Government as the site for a library to house his private memorabilia and presidential papers. Later, he bequeathed Springwood and its properties to the government as well and today they are administered by the National Park Service.

The landscape at Springwood runs down to the Hudson. It is heavily treed and has a very rural feeling. I've drawn the east facade of the large house, excluding the stone wings on either side, in order to focus on the details of the central brick core.

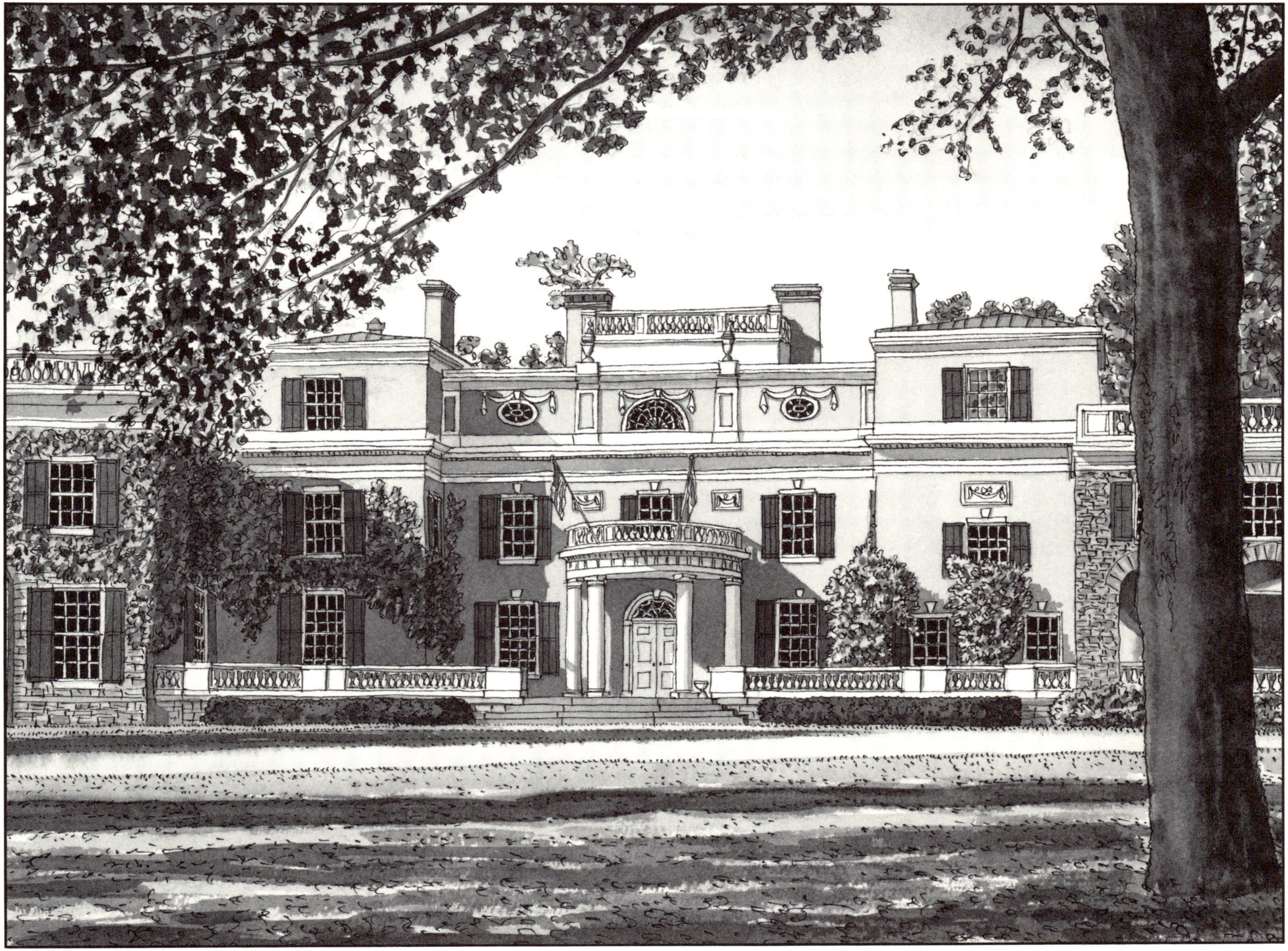

Crawford House

Crawford House, home of the Orange County Historical Society, was built in 1830 by David Crawford, a naval captain who brought freight steamboats to the Hudson and helped make Newburgh a 19th century center of commerce. The house is a wood frame Greek Revival building of grand proportions with four large columns under a high pedimented portico. It is located in the Montgomery Street Historic District and commands panoramic views of Newburgh Bay.

I like this building very much and tried in the drawing of its east facade to re-capture the atmosphere of Newburgh at its peak of commerce and maritime activity. The drawing was made on a bright winter's day during the holiday season.

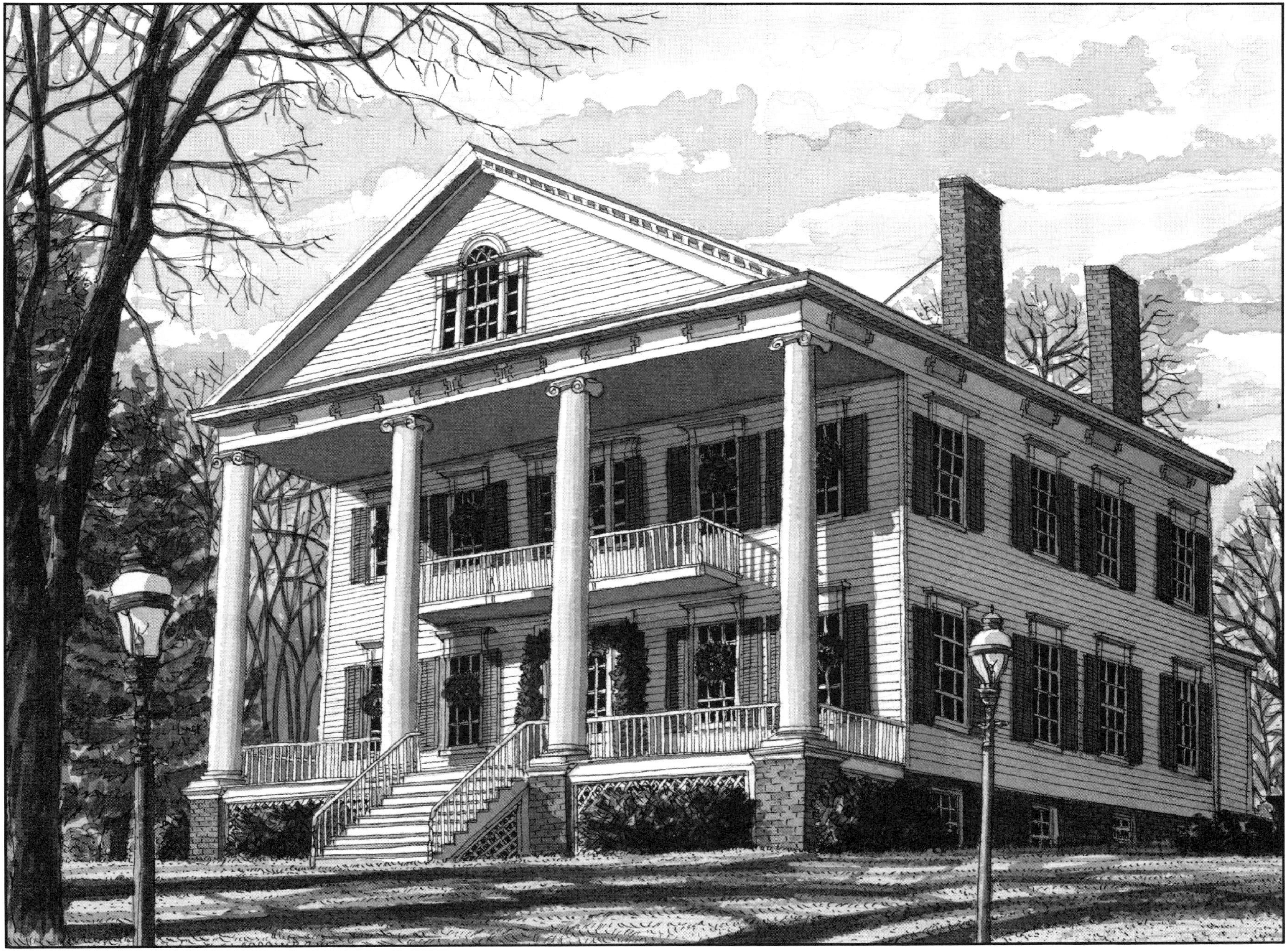

LOCUST GROVE

Samuel F.B. Morse, the distinguished portrait painter who is best known for his invention of the telegraph, purchased Locust Grove in 1847 to serve as a country residence and ornamental farm. Morse commissioned the architect-landscape gardener Alexander Jackson Davis to re-design the existing house, built in 1830, in the style of a Tuscan Villa. Morse's choice of the Italian Renaissance as architectural inspiration grew out of his love for the Italian countryside. His careful attention to the design of the gardens and the critical acclaim they attracted during his lifetime are evidence of his abiding fascination with the landscape.

Locust Grove was acquired by William H. Young just after the turn of the century and a dining room was added on the north side of the house. During the following decades Martha Innis Young assembled an impressive collection of American furnishings and objets d'art. In 1975 her daughter endowed a trust to maintain the estate and its collections as an historic site and wildlife sanctuary.

I chose to sketch the south facade of the house because it incorporates the most representational elements of the structure -- the tower, porte cochere and octagonal south wing -- and because stands of trees growing close to the house on all other sides obscured the view. (In this view I visually erased just one large tree.) The sun in the south provided welcome light for winter drawing.

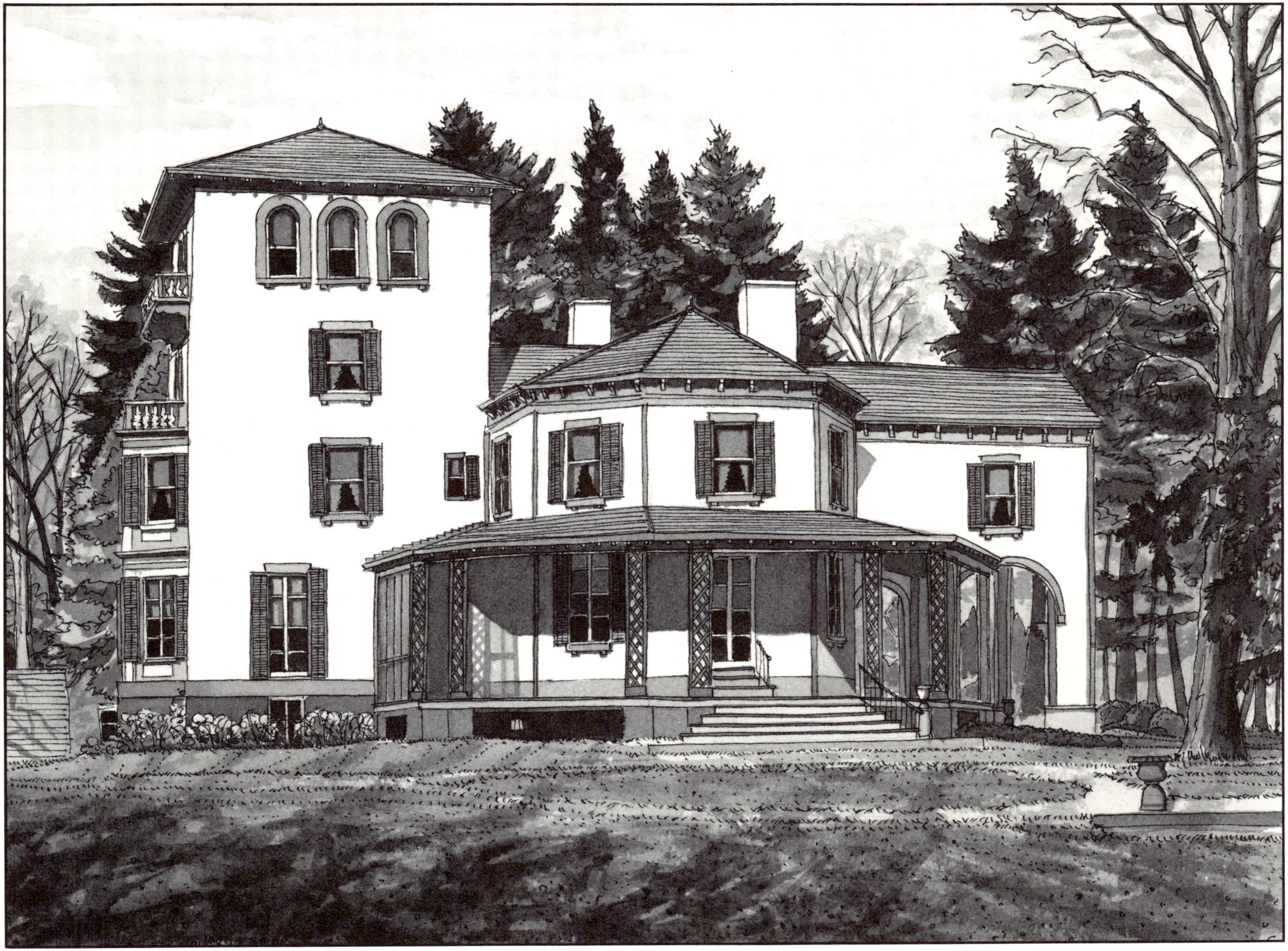

35 JACOB BLAUVELT HOUSE

When Jacob J. Blauvelt built this handsome red brick house in 1832, his family had already occupied the farmlands on which it stood for four generations. The house is an interesting example of rural Hudson River Valley architecture that combines several popular styles of the time. The gambrel roof is in the Dutch style, the doorways and interior details are inspired by Federal and Greek Revival styles.

The original house consisted of a kitchen outbuilding and a large west wing. Jacob added a connecting dining wing and his descendants made further additions in the late 19th and early 20th centuries. The Blauvelt House was owned and occupied by family members until 1970, when it was acquired by the Historical Society of Rockland County. Under the auspices of that organization it has been restored to its early 19th century appearance.

The house is located in a semi-rural setting and has retained much of its original flavor, thanks to the many large trees on the property. The barn complex on the north side suggests how life was lived in a typical 19th century farmhouse. This drawing shows the south facade.

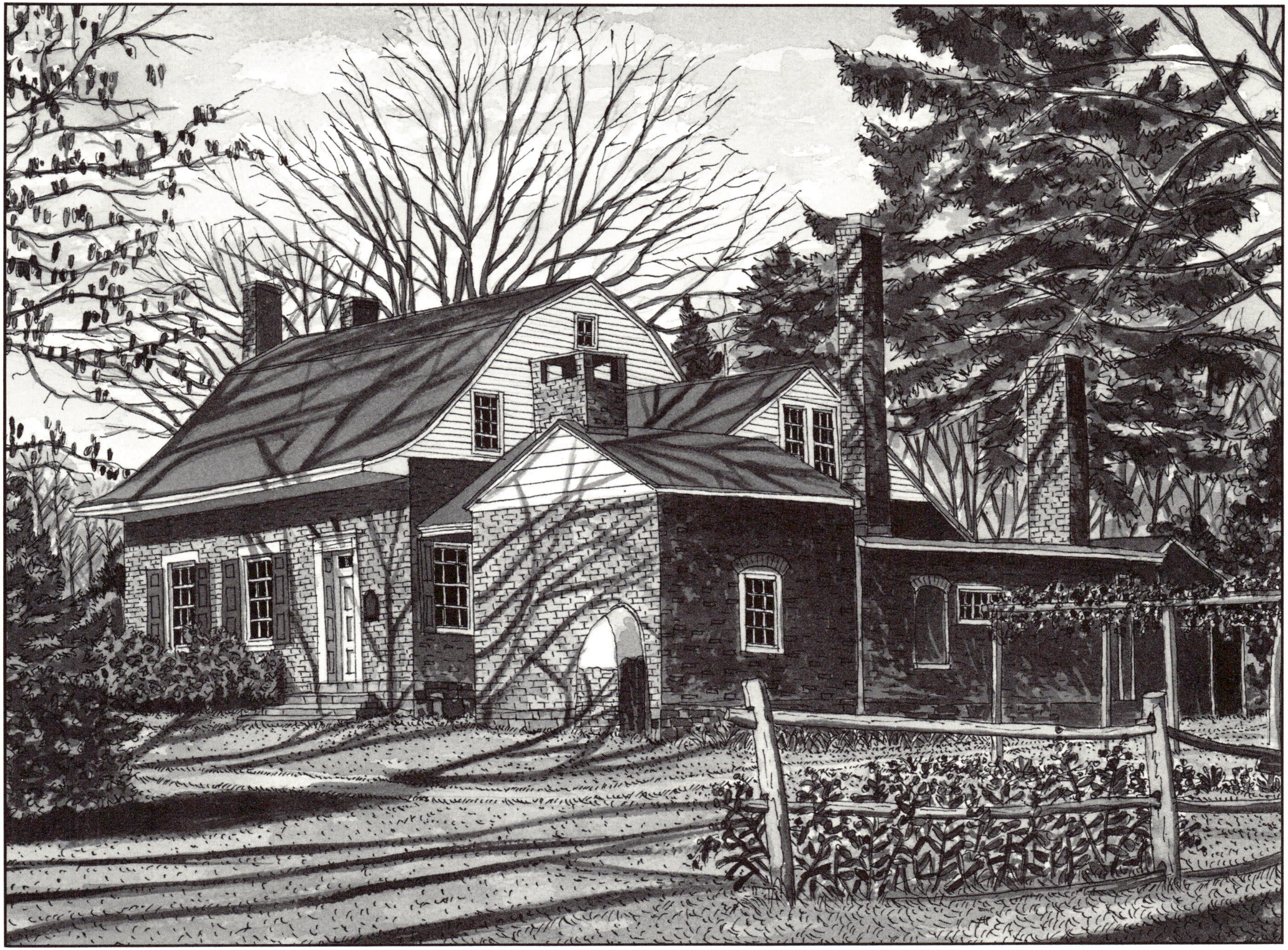

Sunnyside

"A little old-fashioned stone mansion, all made up of gable ends and as full of angles and corners as an old cocked hat" is how Washington Irving described his idiosyncratic estate in Tarrytown. He bought the simple stone Dutch farmhouse in 1832 and, with the assistance of landscape painter George Harvey, romanticized it into one of the most endearing houses in the Hudson Valley.

Sunnyside acquired its pagoda-like tower in 1847. The wisteria that Irving planted at the front door is still splendid today. Irving lived here until his death in 1859. During his lifetime the house was a popular port of call for writers and other creative people from around the world.

Sunnyside is a complex building to capture on paper. I chose to draw the south facade because it shows the main mass of the building to best advantage.

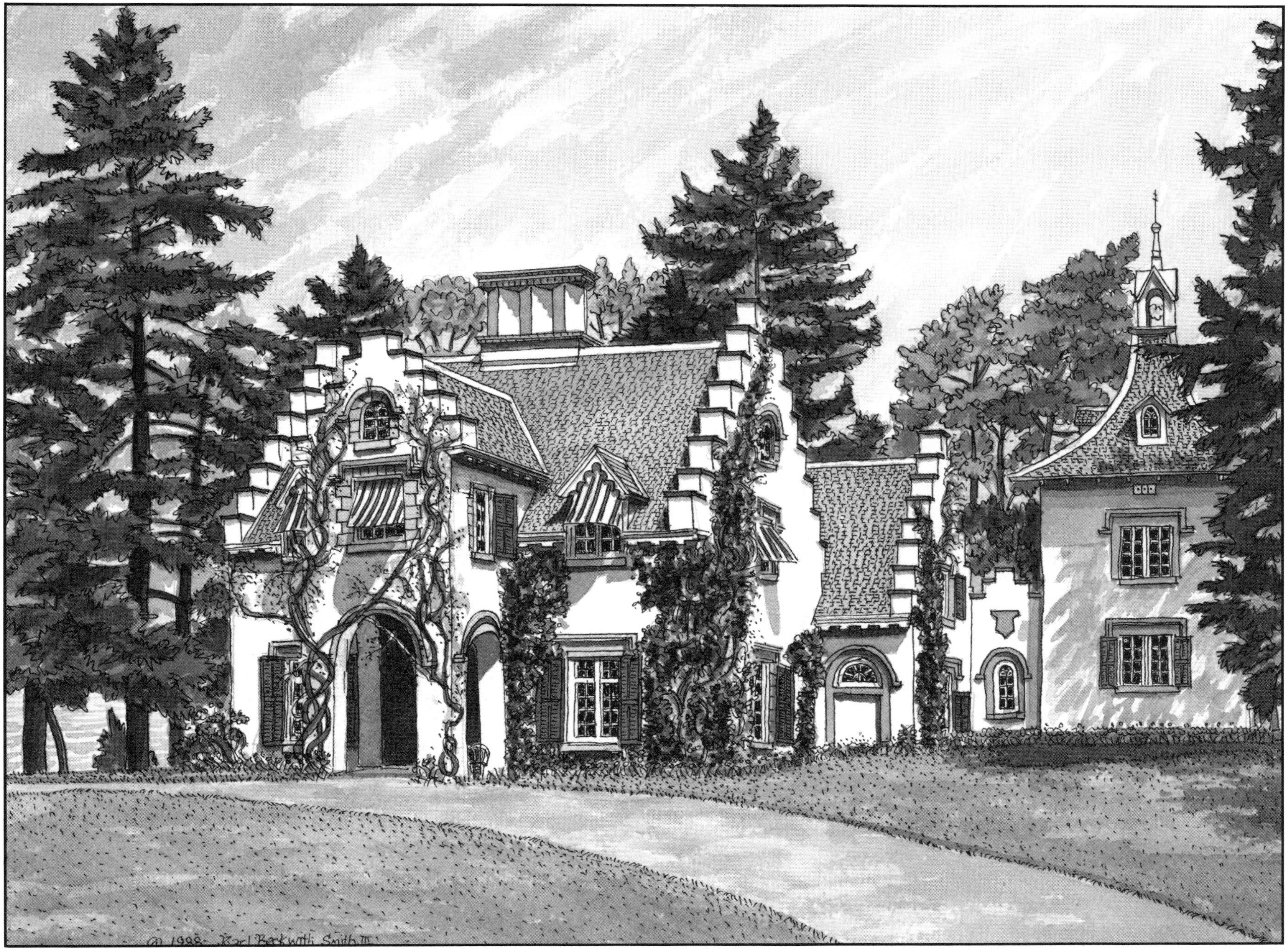
© 1988 - Karl Beckwith Smith III

LYNDHURST

Lyndhurst is widely recognized as the finest Gothic Revival residence in America. It was designed by the master of that genre, Alexander Jackson Davis. He created the initial dwelling in 1838 for New York City Mayor General William Paulding and a vast addition in 1865 for George Merritt, its second owner.

The house is built of brick faced with Ossining marble. It boasts a four storey tower, turrets, diamond shaped windows that overlook the river, an elegant porte cochere and an expansive veranda. The interior is finished in densely crenellated, handcrafted woodwork.

Financier Jay Gould purchased Lyndhurst in 1881 and built an extraordinary greenhouse on the grounds over 375 feet long, plus wings. The skeleton of that structure still stands. In 1900 specimens from the greenhouse established the orchid collection at the New York Botanical Garden. Lyndhurst was given by Gould heirs in 1964 to the National Trust for Historic Preservation.

I find it interesting that, in spite of its massive scale, Lyndhurst is not at all foreboding. That is due largely to the beautiful pale colors of its marble exterior -- whites, off-whites and tones of pink. Unlike the granite and wood buildings of the region that blend into the landscape, Lyndhurst seems to blend into the sky and clouds. I sketched this view of the east facade on a crystal clear spring day.

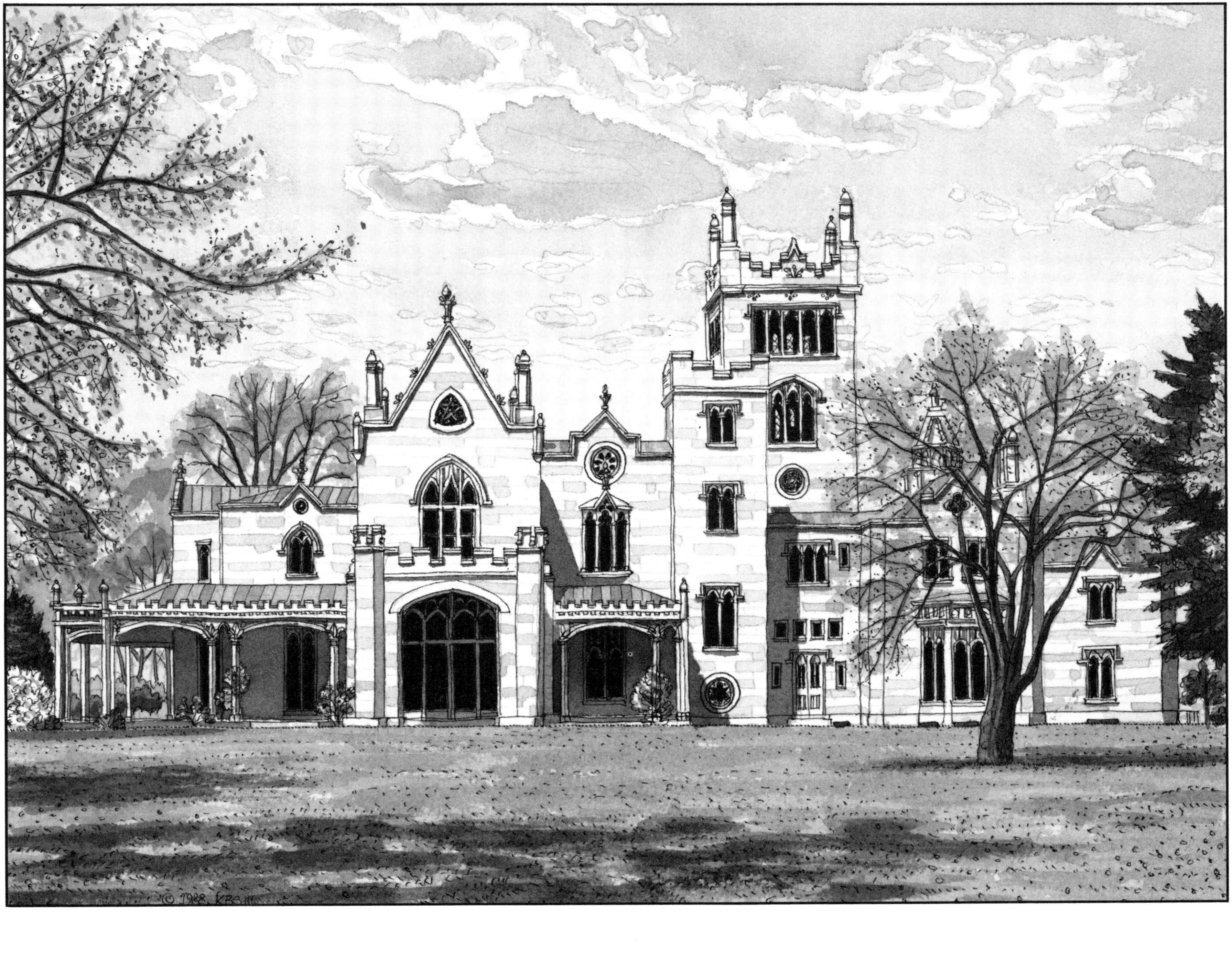
© 1988

DELAMATER HOUSE

This wood cottage, designed by Alexander Jackson Davis and built in 1844, is a little gem in the 'carpenter gothic' style. It is characterized by a central gable, gingerbread woodwork, diamond-paned windows, over-tall chimney stacks and projecting bay windows.

The house is now owned by the Beekman Arms, an historic inn in the town of Rhinebeck.

I found it a challenge and pleasure to try and capture the intricate detail of the woodwork and the terra cotta ornament on the chimneys of this very romantic house.

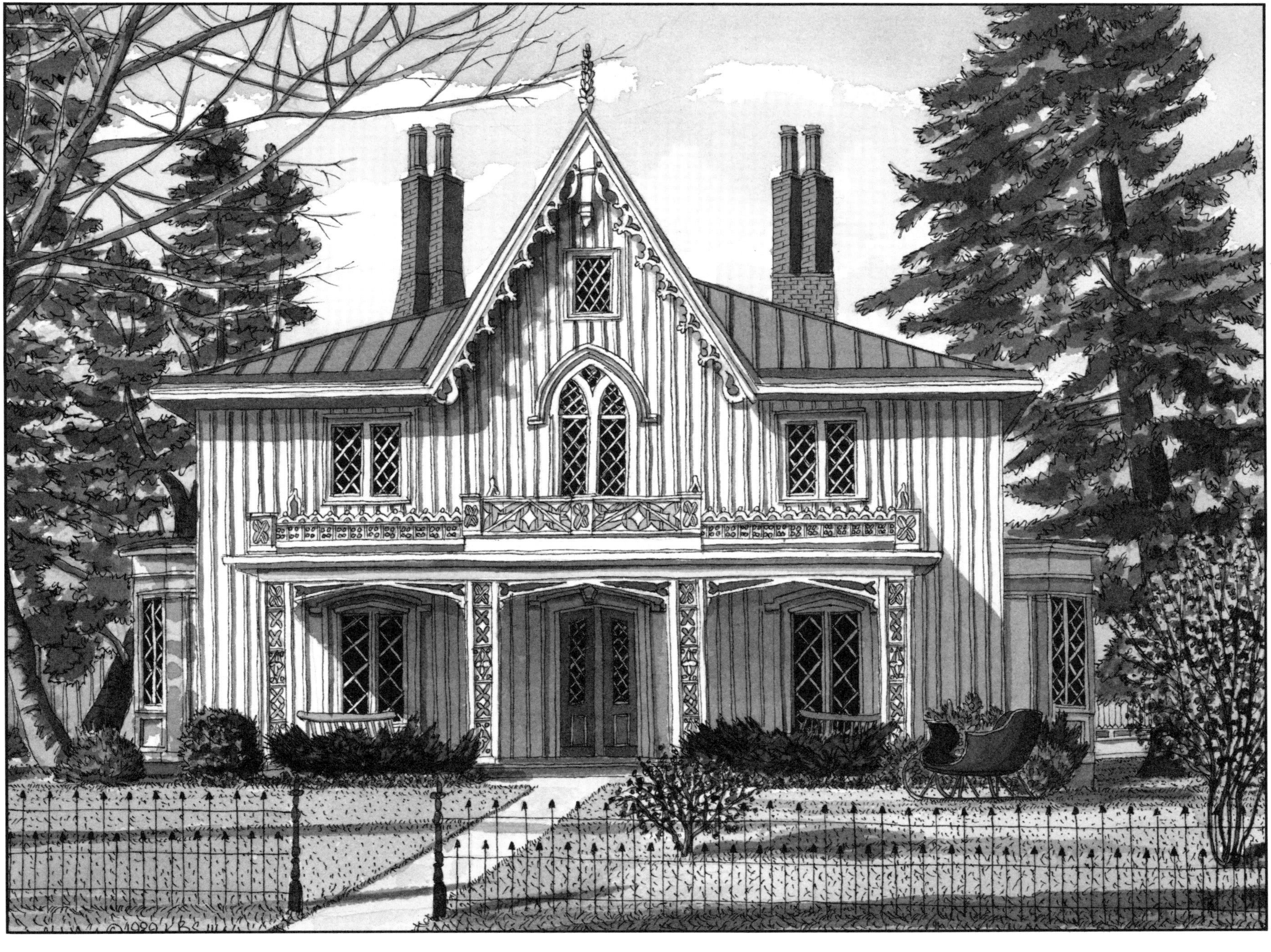

WILDERSTEIN

Thomas Holy Suckley built Wilderstein, an adaptation of the Queen Anne style, in 1852. Thirty five years later, Poughkeepsie architect, Arnout Cannon, enlarged it to its present size and noted landscape architect, Calvert Vaux, designed the grounds which sweep to the Hudson. In the 1890's a group of outbuildings, including a gardener's lodge, carriage house and two Adirondack style gazebos, were added to the property. Interior details of the house were designed by J.B. Tiffany.

Since its groundbreaking, Wilderstein has been owned by the Suckley family. A third generation family member currently resides there and has established Wilderstein Preservation, a non-profit organization dedicated to preserving the estate.

Wilderstein is clad in unpainted, weathered wood that reminds me of an old ship. I have drawn the west facade of the house which looks out to the river.

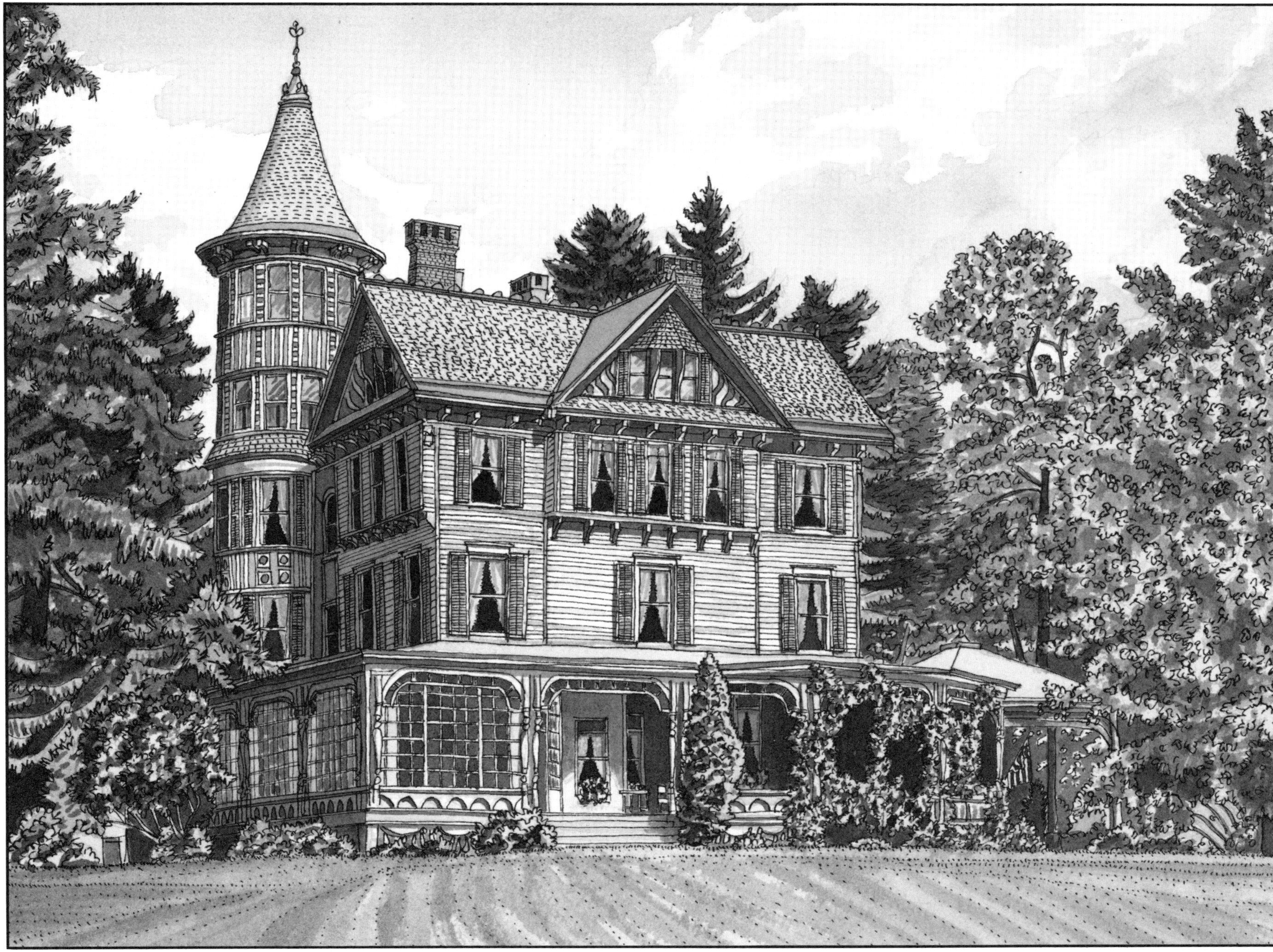

The Malcolm Gordon School

The Malcolm Gordon School, located on a bluff overlooking Constitution Marsh and the Hudson River, was built as a summer house in 1854 for William Moore and his wife, Margaret Philipse Gouveneur. The yellow brick, Gothic style structure was designed by architect Richard Upjohn for William Moore. In 1927 it was purchased by the Gordon family who established the school that still operates on the site.

The Malcolm Gordon School is a fine example of domestic architecture of the mid 19th century as it has remained virtually unchanged since its early days. The bay window, porch and slightly arched windows are particularly pleasing details. This building is the center of social life at the school. The scene that greeted me on one visit, of headmaster and boys gathered in its main room after dinner, seemed timeless and might as easily have been taking place in the past century as in the present.

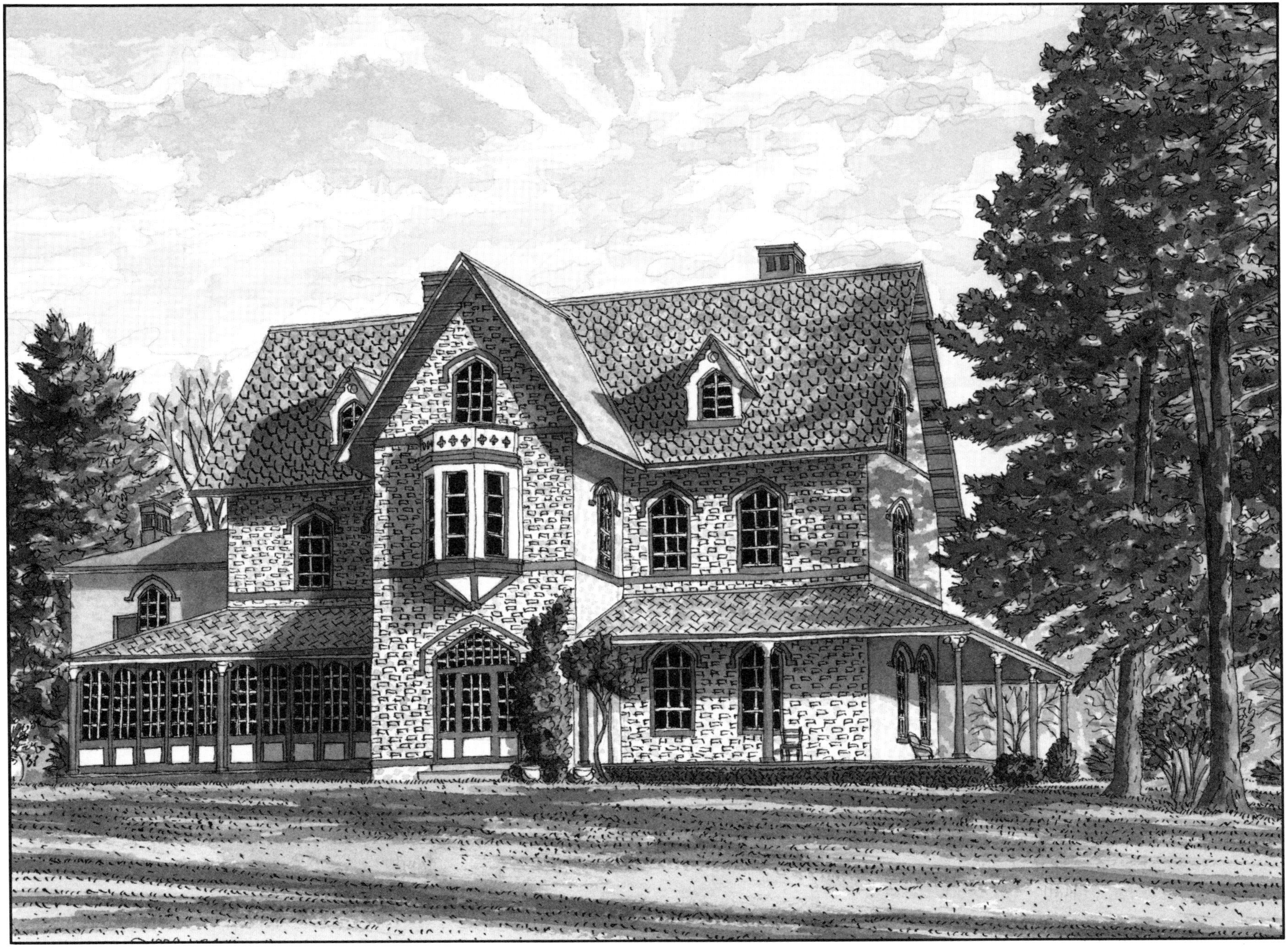

41 ROSSITER HOUSE

Thomas Rossiter was a Hudson River painter who shared with several other important artists living in the Hudson River Valley a deep love of Italian architecture and landscape design. Rossiter designed this country house himself. (He lived permanently in New York City in an Italian Renaissance home designed by Richard Morris Hunt.)

Built in 1860, Rossiter House takes its inspiration from the houses of Florence and Venice, with classical cornices and a tower on the east side, a beautiful colonnade on the ground floor and a broad veranda-like porch on the second level. The brick with stucco building is situated on one of the most beautiful sites on the river, just south of Cold Spring. Today it is a carefully maintained private residence.

When I think of the quintessential Hudson villa this one comes to mind both because of its architecture and its setting. Rossiter House sits like a wedding cake on top of a hill. The view from the house encompasses sheep in the meadows, Constitution Marsh and the river as far south as the Bear Mountain Bridge. I made this drawing while sitting in the meadow with the river at my back.

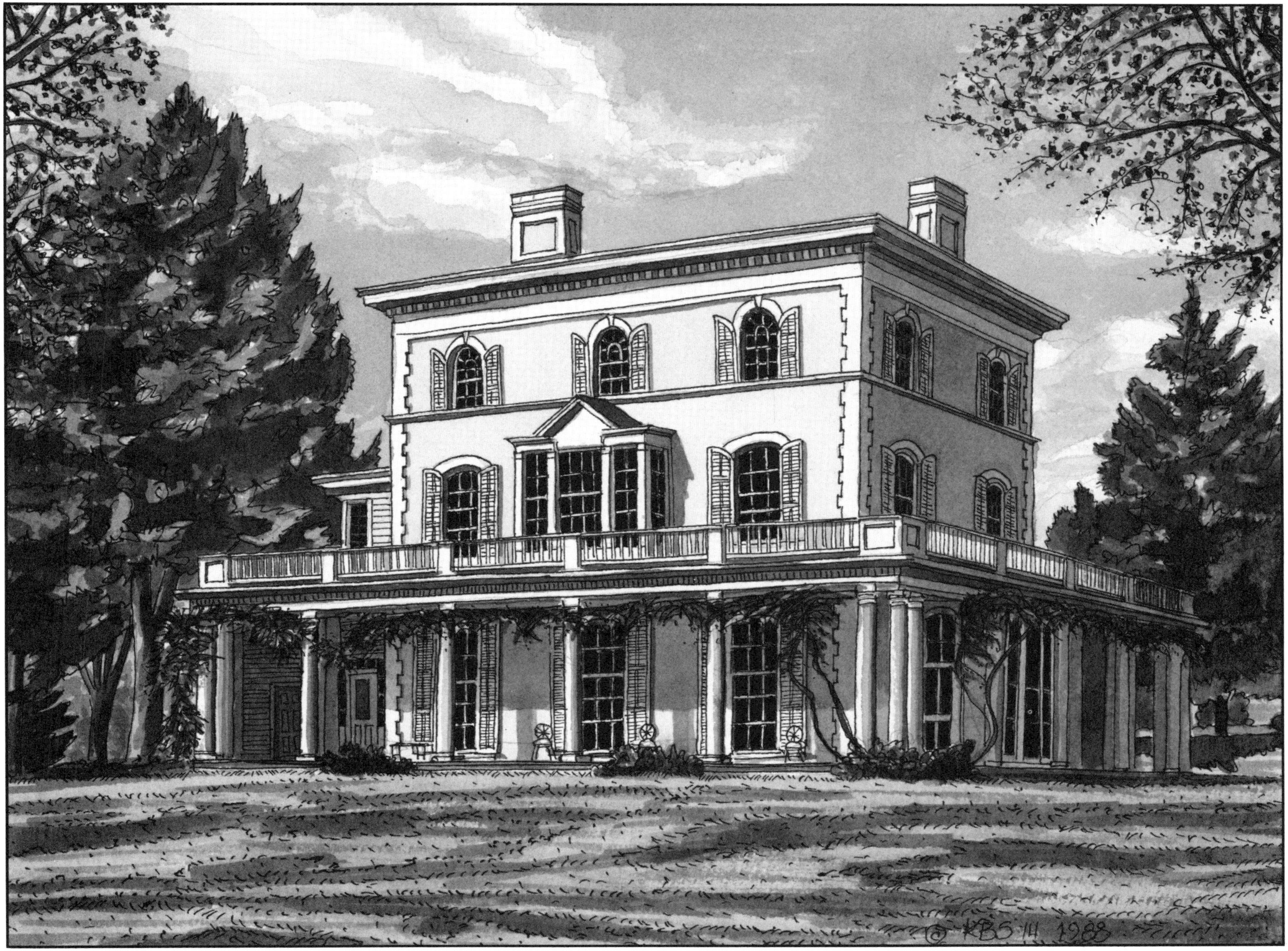
© KBS III 1988

Mohonk Mountain House

This Victorian stone resort hotel stands 1200 feet above the Rondout Valley on the edge of Mohonk Lake. It was built by twin brothers, Albert and Alfred Smiley, in 1870 -- the heyday of the extravagant and elegant country hotel. In that same year the railroad was completed to New Paltz and construction began on the Old Stage Road, one of a series of new carriage roads that would be built by the end of the century.

Mohonk Mountain House is a rambling assemblage of buildings set on 1500 acres of land. Many additions and outbuildings have been constructed in the more than one hundred years since the rustic log-style main structure was erected. Its extensive gardens, specimen trees, walking and bridle paths and protected natural surroundings are the legacy of a Quaker family with an early interest in conservation.

I found Mohonk so large, with its many wings and additions in so many styles, that it was hard to capture in detail. Instead, I've concentrated on showing the mass of the building in relation to its majestic setting.

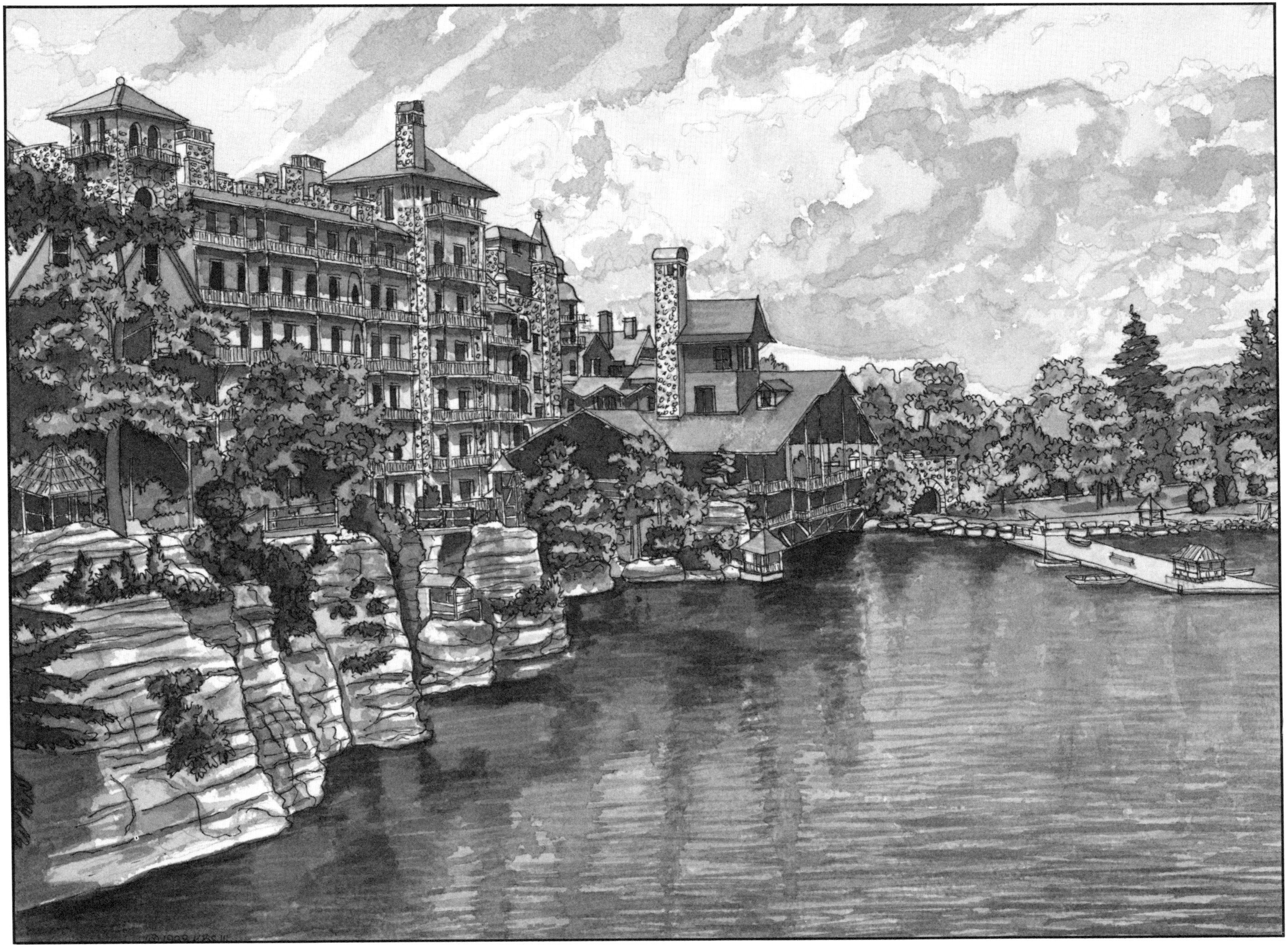

OLANA

Frederick Church earned his reputation as one of 19th century America's most important landscape painters but Olana is his masterpiece -- a total triumph of architecture, painting, landscaping and interior decoration. For years the artist sought the perfect location on the river on which to build a home and it was while living in a farm cottage designed by Richard Morris Hunt that he found his perfect hill top and began his grand scheme.

In 1870 architect Calvert Vaux registered the first plans for the structure and, although he remained the official architect on the project, Olana is without question Church's own creation. The style of the house was influenced by the artist's travels in the middle east. He called it "personal Persian." Its walls are of two and one half feet thick rough stone that was quarried on the site. A tower, turrets, colored brick laid in patterns, mosaics, painted cornices and brightly colored and gilt slate roof tiles are among the most arresting of its exterior features.

The interior of the house is designed around a central courtroom, in the Persian manner, and the rooms that radiate from it are decorated with Church's own polychromed paintings and stencils, scores of his canvasses and thousands of artifacts, from baskets to framed butterflies, from Shaker chairs to a gilded Buddha.

The house took twenty years to complete and in the final years Church added a working studio. His descendants inhabited the home until it was purchased by the state in 1967 after a broad-based effort to save it from the auction block. This view of the south facade shows the tower that is the bejewelled lid to the box.

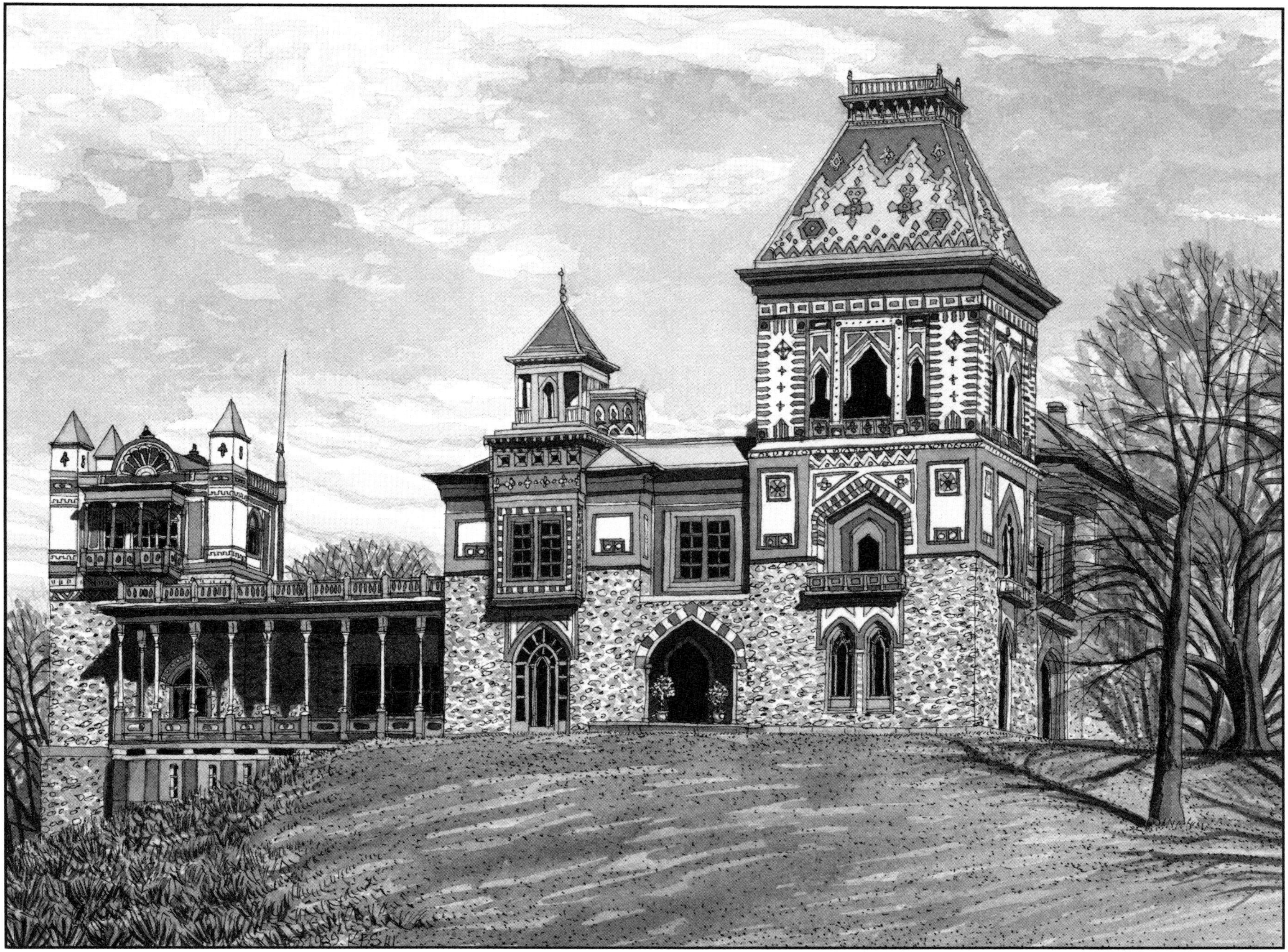

Albany City Hall

Architect H. H. Richardson was working on the New York State Capitol Building project when the old Albany City Hall burned down. He was promptly given the commission to design a new official building for the city and the result is one of his most Romanesque creations. The ubiquitous arches of City Hall are embellished with tiers of relief sculpture and gargoyles that are barely discernible from a distance. The same stonecarvers who worked on the Capitol building were called into service here.

The door and window openings of the building are given depth through the contrast of rough granite surfaces and brownstone trim. The narrowness of the vertically-slotted windows give the building an austere feeling.

Albany City Hall is a perfect example of the grandiose public architecture that was characteristic of the late 19th century and the years of this century until the Great Depression. The drawing depicts its west facade and in order to express the full mass of the structure is, by necessity, something of a miniature.

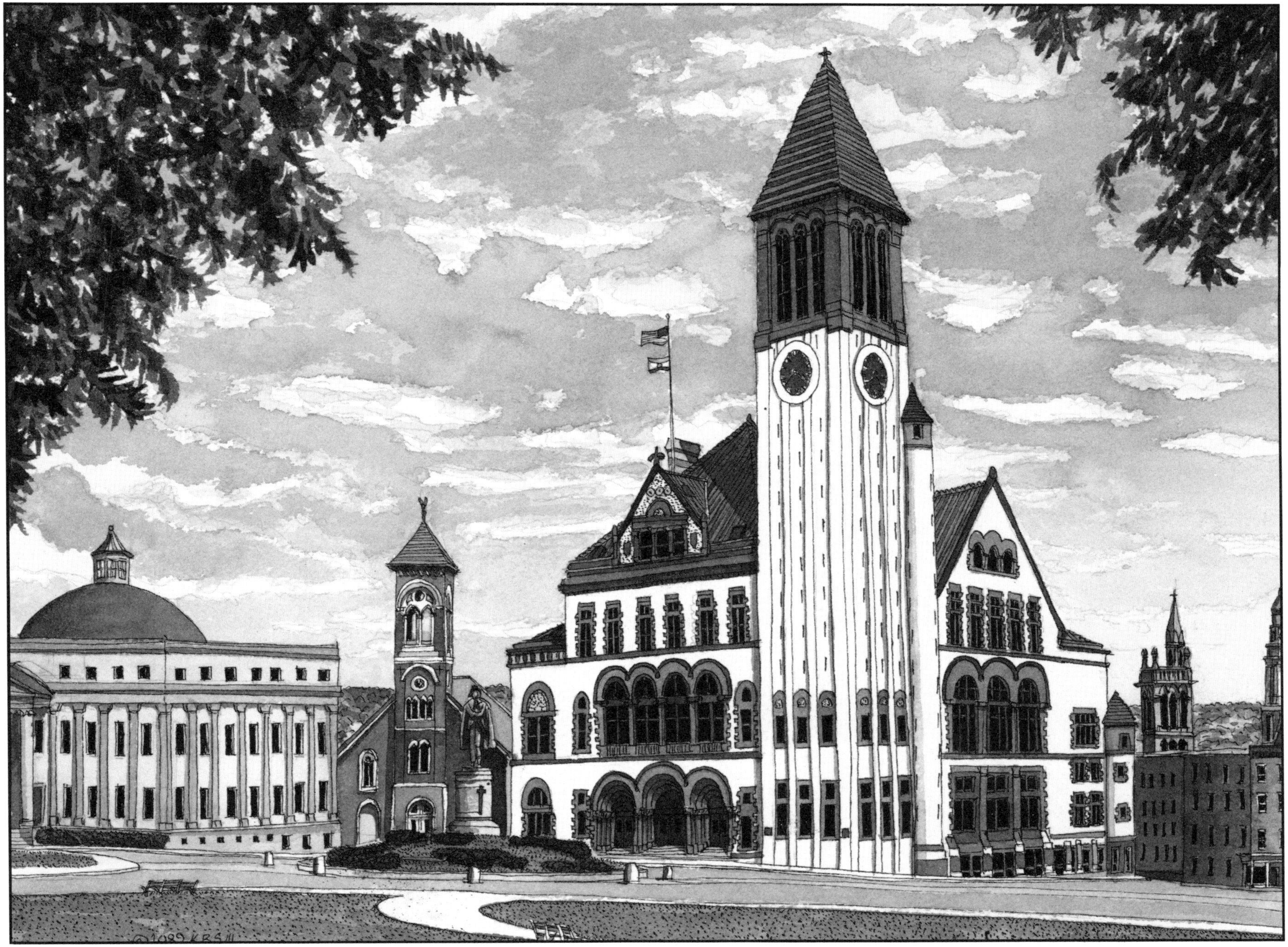
©1989 KBS II

Estherwood

Estherwood, a mansion in the style of the French Chateau, was built in 1895 by James Jennings McComb. The inspiration for the structure was an octagonal desk he had purchased in Europe some years earlier. McComb hired Buchman and Deisler, architects, to design a residence on a grand scale around a library housing the desk.

The ornate, three and one half storey mansion is constructed of white pressed brick and trimmed with Jonesville granite. The profuse terra cotta exterior ornament represented an important innovation. Buchman and Deisler were commercial architects and, at Estherwood, they applied this heretofore commercial material in a sumptuous residential setting. Estherwood possesses typical romantic features of the chateau style: a porte cochere, tiled and mosaic-floored veranda, tower with copper cupola and glass conservatory. This handsome structure now houses The Masters School.

The drawing of the south facade shows the striations and gradations of color in the stone on the ground floor and the detail of the incredible tile roof.

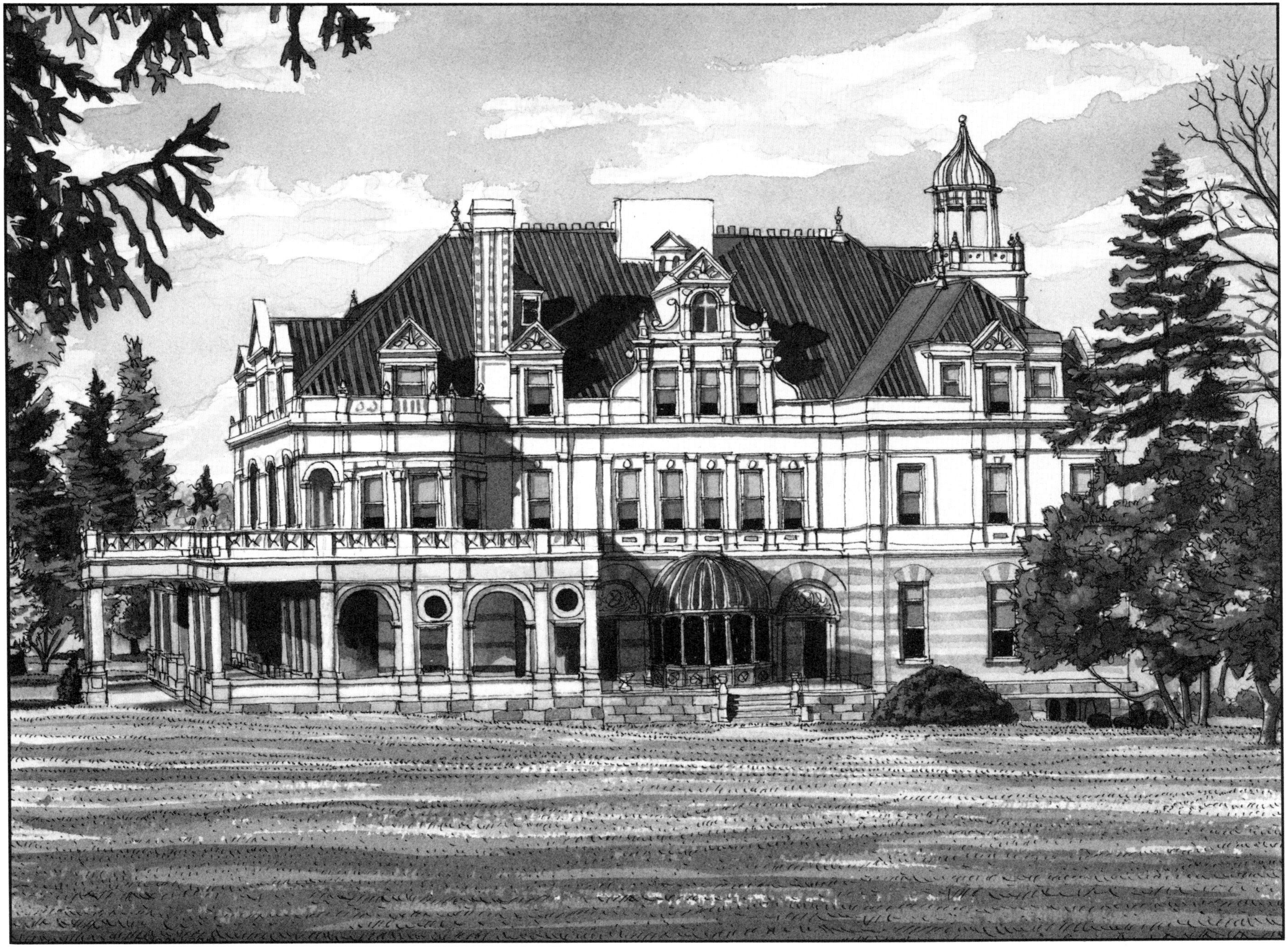

MILLS MANSION

The first house to occupy the site on which the Mills Mansion now stands was a red brick farmhouse built in the 1790's by Gertrude Livingston and her husband, Morgan Lewis, who was later to become governor of New York. When the house burned in 1832 the Lewises built a new home on the site in the popular Greek Revival style.

By the end of the 19th century the estate had been occupied by several generations of Livingstons and was owned by Ruth and Ogden Mills. In 1895 they commissioned McKim, Mead and White to enlarge the mansion in the manner of the grand country residences being erected by other leading American families up and down the river.

The New York architects created a neoclassic Beaux-Arts mansion of brick with a white stucco facade. Two large wings were added and the exterior gained fluted columns, pilasters and ornate swags. Its sixty-five rooms were decorated in the styles of Louis XV and Louis XVI: they are panelled, gilded, marbled and carved. The Mills Mansion remained in Livingston family hands until it was given, in 1938, to the State of New York.

I chose to depict the west facade of the mansion, as the east facade is very similar to that of the Vanderbilt Mansion, another McKim, Mead and White design. The facade shown faces the river and has a large terrace at its center, rather than the traditional portico. The canvas tent shown in the drawing was set up for a special event. I think it adds something to the drawing by suggesting the quality of life in such a place.

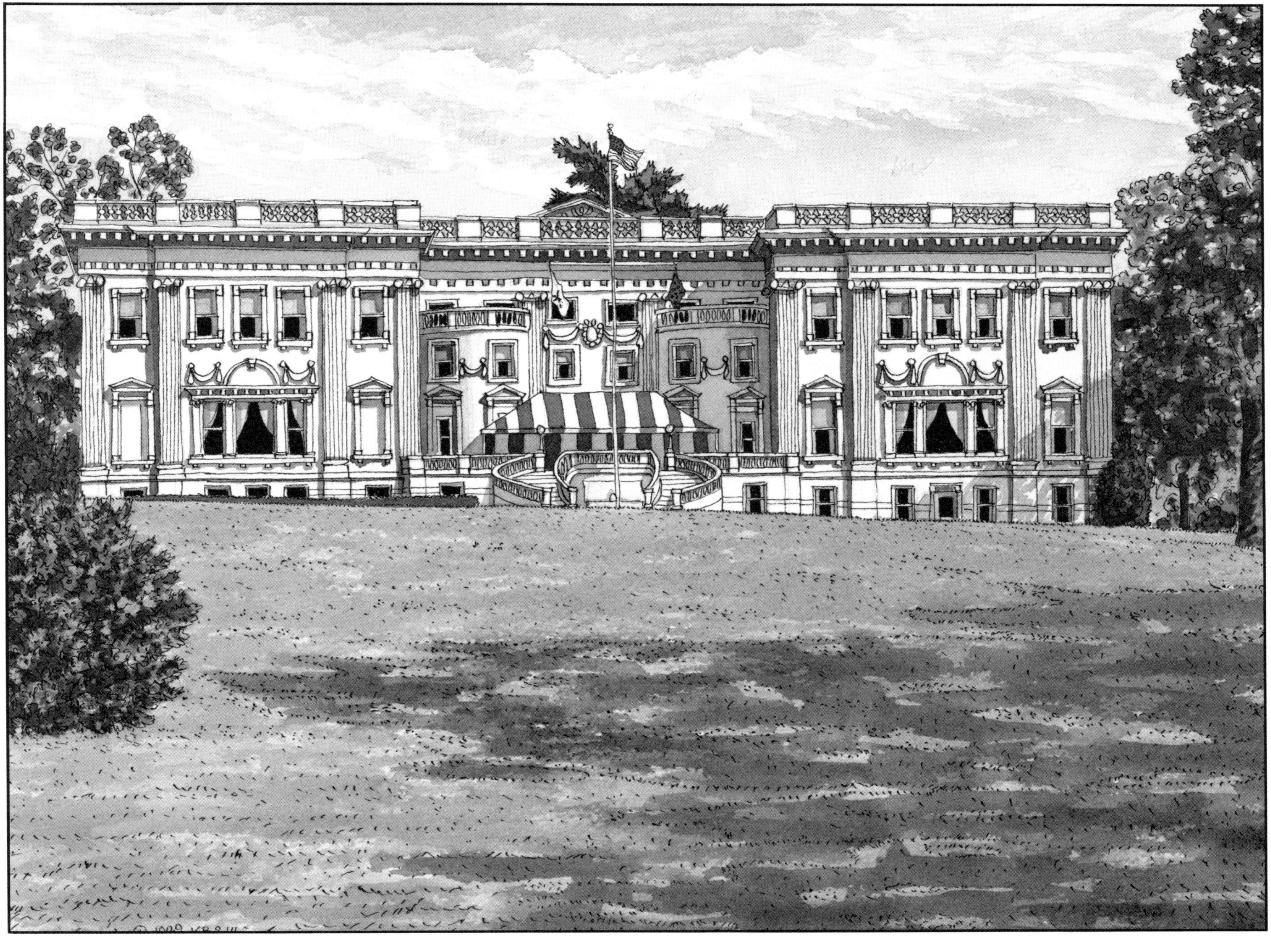

New York State Capitol

For more than thirty years five architects, legions of journeymen and more than six hundred stonecarvers labored to create the architectural extravaganza that is the New York State Capitol building. The first designs for the building were begun by architect Thomas Fuller in 1867. The Assembly Chamber, designed by architect Leopold Eidlitz, was added during the years between 1876 and 1879. In 1881 H.H. Richardson designed the Senate Chamber and, with Isaac G. Perry, the great western stair, often called "the million dollar staircase."

The first floor of the building is Italian Renaissance, the second and third are transitional, the fourth, Romanesque and the fifth, French Renaissance. The granite structure is embellished inside and out with portraiture of great Americans, characters from literature, birds, beasts and mythological figures.

In 1978 the Senate created a temporary commission on the restoration of the capitol. The effort to strip the building of a century of architectural obfuscation and return it to its once great splendor is still in progress.

Despite the architectural, political and economic imbroglios associated with its construction, the State Capitol stands as a very impressive building and, by far, the most interesting one in the Empire State Plaza. In this view of the south facade, drawn from the vantage point of the reflecting pools in the Plaza, I chose to leave out the modern buildings that flank it on either side and detract somewhat from its enjoyment.

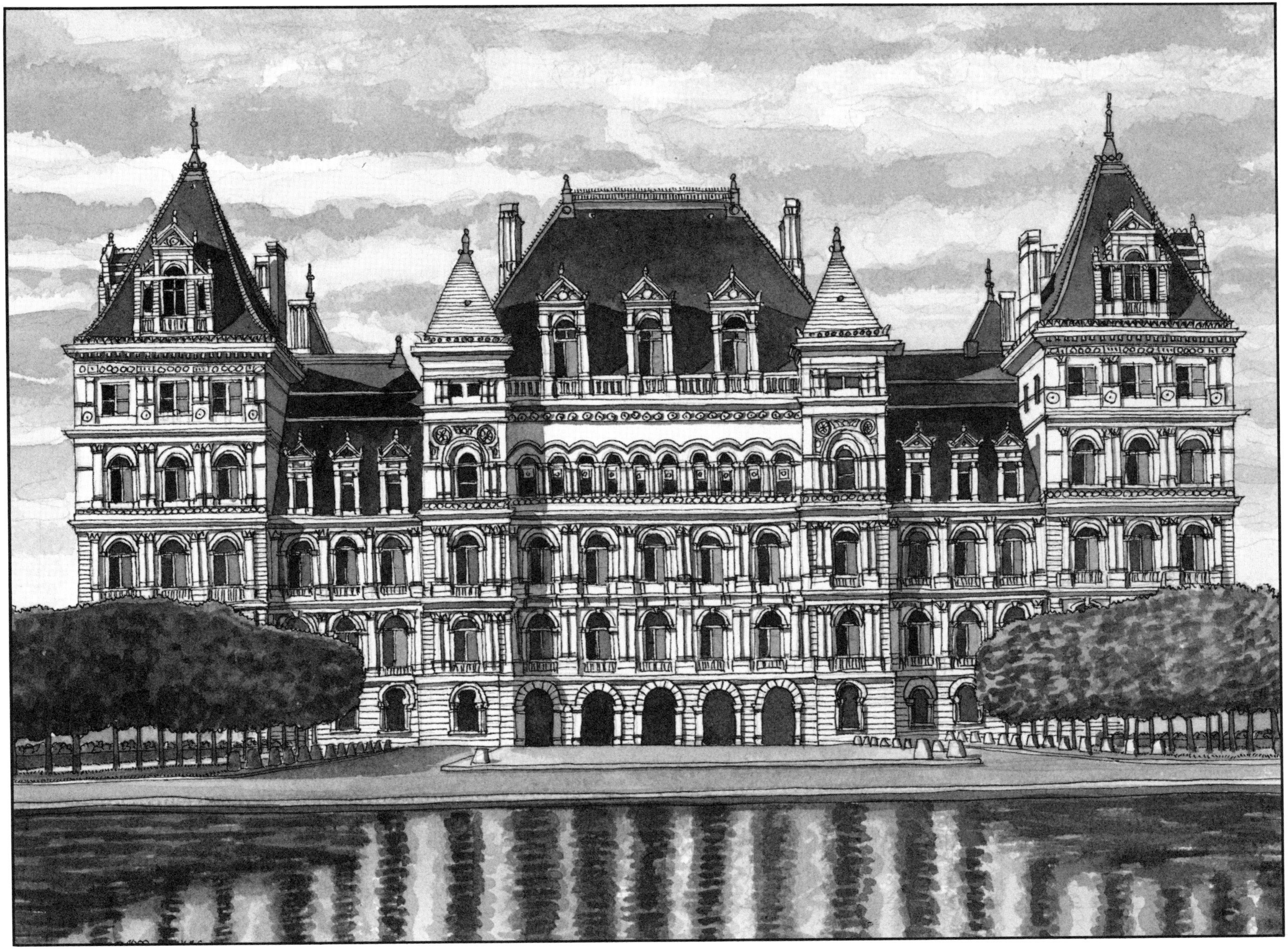

Vanderbilt Mansion

The celebrated architectural firm of McKim, Mead & White designed this most lavish of Hudson River mansions in 1895 for Frederick W. Vanderbilt, grandson of "The Commodore." Construction took four years and was completed in 1899. Vanderbilt Mansion is a fifty room Italian Renaissance palace, built of Indiana limestone and elaborately detailed, inside and out. The mansion was used by the Vanderbilt family during the spring and fall social seasons. Its Italian and French baroque interiors were designed by Georges Glaenzer and Ogden Codman Jr.

The two-hundred-plus acre property on which the mansion stands had been developed long before the Vanderbilts selected it as a site for their own residence. In 1764 Dr. John Bard built the first house on the land and his son, Samuel, followed with a house of his own. Samuel's house was later enlarged and remodeled by several owners, including John Jacob Astor. In 1845 it burned to the ground. Dorothea Langdon, Astor's daughter, erected a forty room Greek Revival home on the site but, when the Vanderbilts acquired the property in 1895, they tore it down to make way for construction of a more palatial domain.

Dr. Bard planned the first plantings on the estate in the mid 18th century and throughout the two centuries that followed successive owners developed the extraordinary landscape. There are forty different specimens of trees planted here (many of them marked) on acreage that rolls down to the river's edge. The Vanderbilt Mansion was donated to the National Park Service in 1940 by a descendant of the family. The drawing shows the east facade of the building, reflected in morning light.

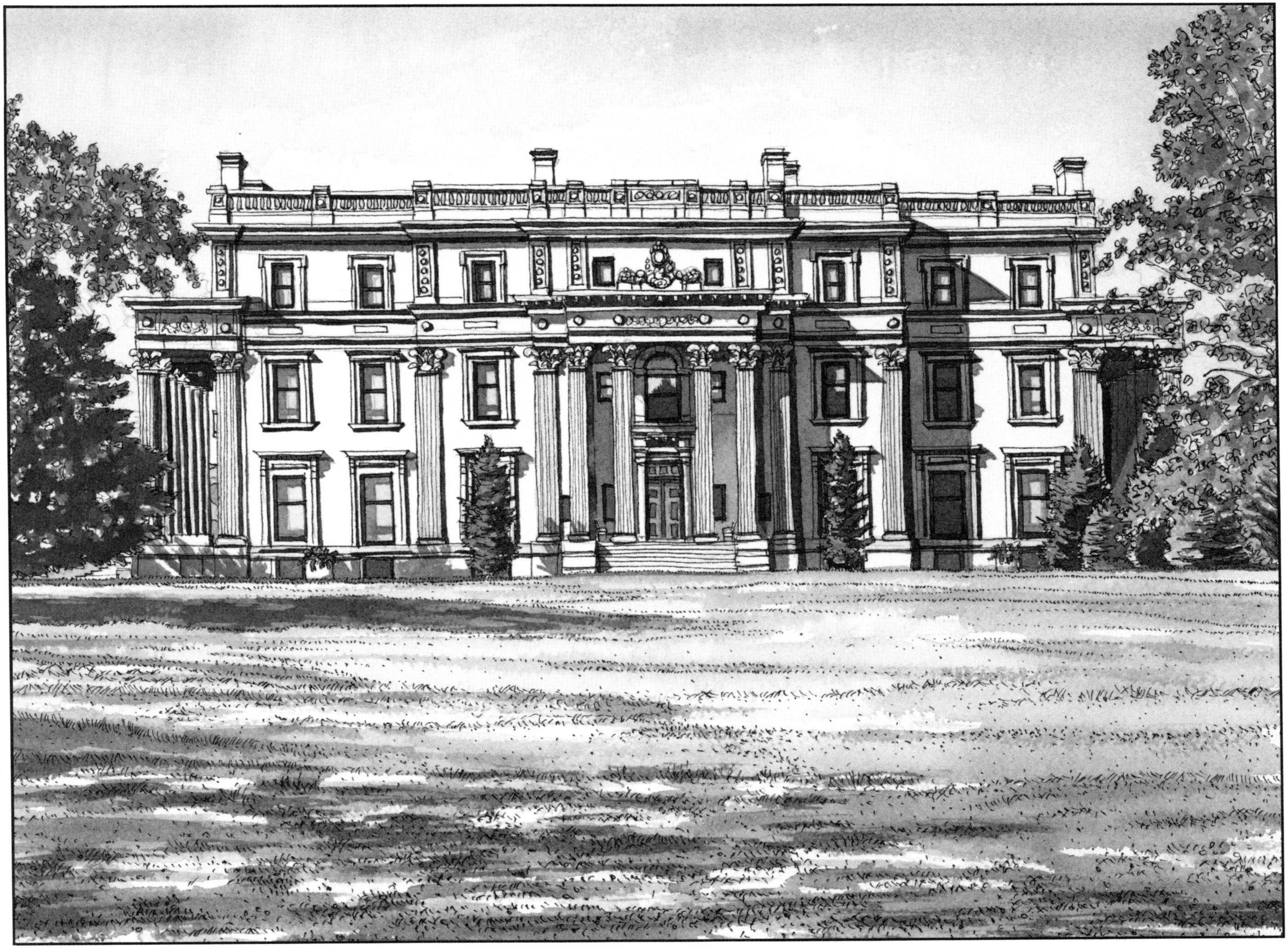

BLITHEWOOD

This Georgian Revival mansion of brick and stucco, designed by architects Hoppin and Koen, was constructed between 1900 and 1901. Captain Andrew C. Zabriskie commissioned the house to be built on the site of Robert Donaldson's Blithewood, an earlier estate that had been remodeled by Alexander Jackson Davis and which Zabriskie tore down in order to carry out his own architectural fantasies.

Blithewood is still called by the name given to Donaldson's estate. It is a name that captures the sense of the sylvan landscape and the wealth of song birds that so impressed the 19th century developers of grand properties in the Hudson Valley. Early in the century the house was surrounded by Italianate gardens but they have since grown over, obscuring the view of the river.

In 1951 the Zabriskie family donated the house to Bard College. It has since been restored and now houses the Jerome Levy Economic Institute.

Blithewood is a turn of the century Beaux Arts extravaganza. I drew the long north facade to convey a sense of the scale of this very large country estate.

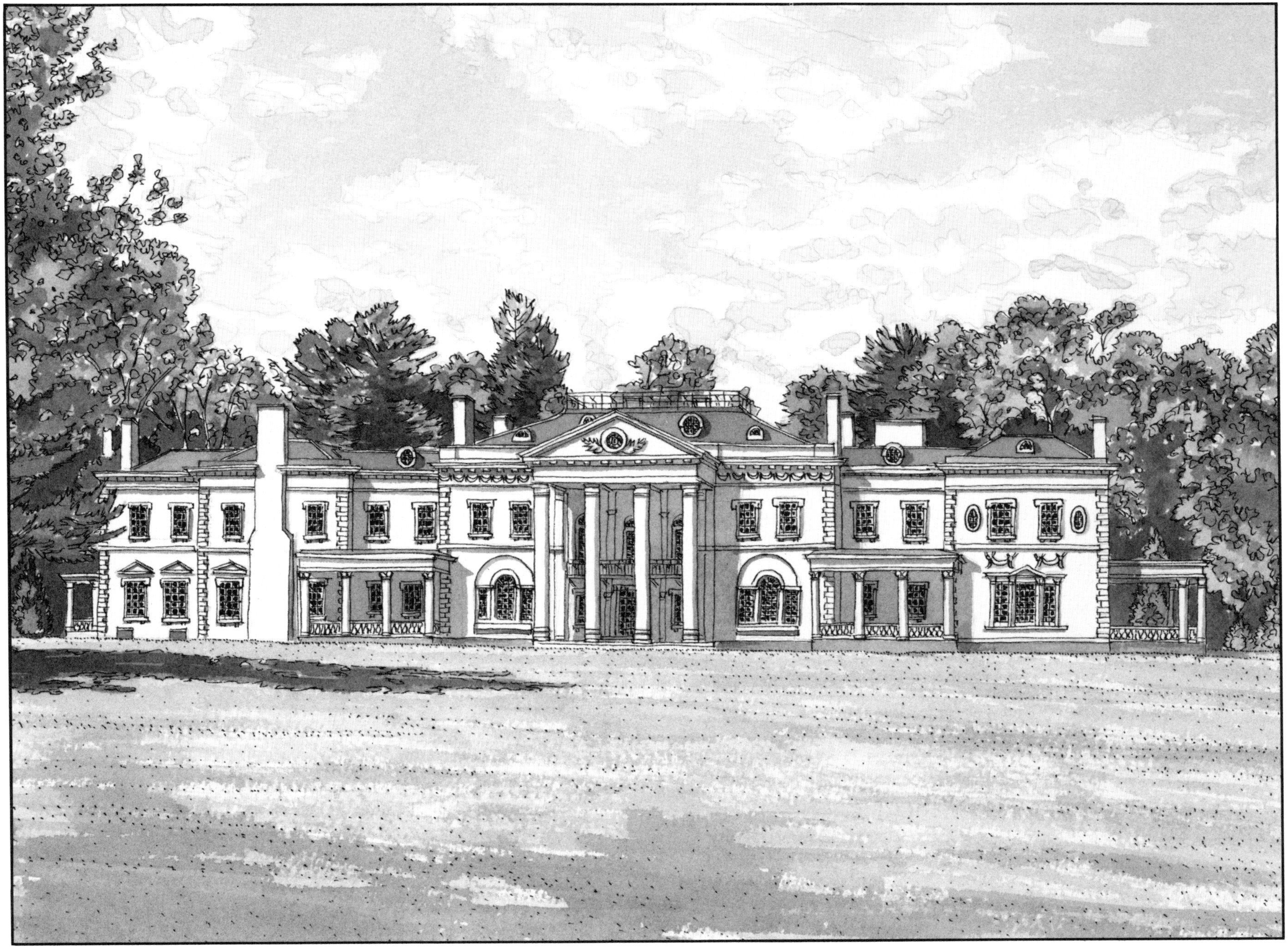

Bannerman's Castle

Bannerman's Castle is a romantic stone ruin overlooking a beautiful stretch of the Hudson just north of the village of Cold Spring. Pollepel Island, on which it stands, was acquired in 1900 by Francis Bannerman VI, an arms merchant who began his career at the age of fourteen when he purchased Civil War surplus arms at auction. Bannerman began building the castle in 1905 to his own design in the baronial style of his native Scotland. Completed in 1918, it served as a summer home and arms storehouse until it was badly damaged by an explosion in 1920.

The Bannerman family continued to use the remaining building as a storehouse until 1967 when the property was added to the Hudson Highlands State Park. A fire in 1969 reduced the castle to its present condition.

Standing on the railroad bed looking toward the river one can look through the ruined building. As I sketched this view of the east facade I watched the light penetrate the huge black masses. Storm King mountain on the opposite shore attracts interesting cloud formations that hang and swirl so there are frequently fierce, stormy clouds behind Bannerman's. The effect is very powerful and dramatic.

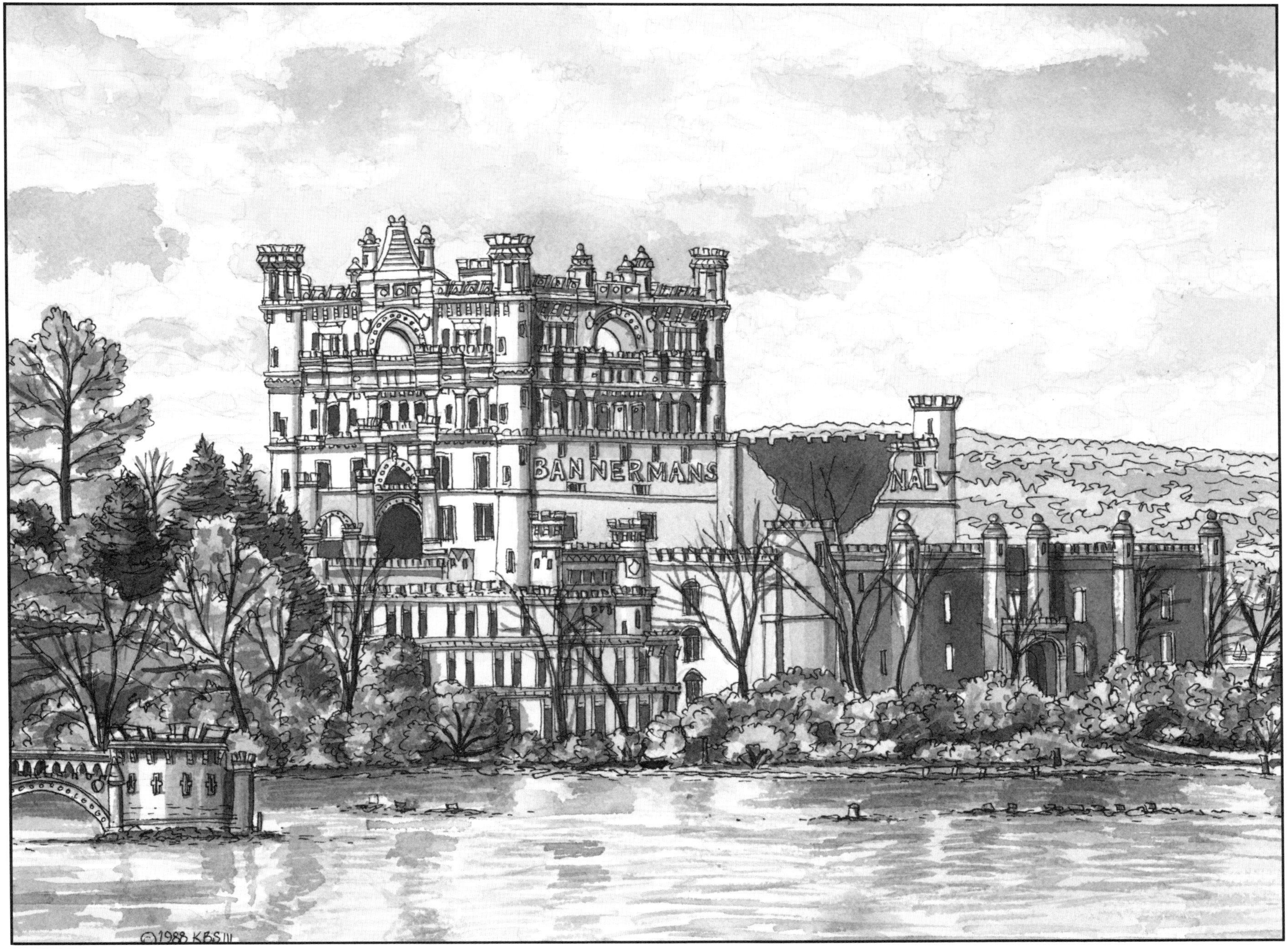
BANNERMANS
NAL
©1988 KBS III

INDEX

PLATE NO.

44	Albany City Hall	46	Mills Mansion
50	Bannerman's Castle	42	Mohonk Mountain House
49	Blithewood	25	Montgomery Place
26	Boscobel	14	Mount Gulian
29	Cedar Grove	19	New Windsor Cantonment
12	Clermont	47	New York State Capitol
20	Clinton House	43	Olana
4	Crailo	2	Old Dutch Church
33	Crawford House	1	Philipsburg Manor Upper Mills
38	Delamater House	10	Philipse Manor Hall
22	DePuy Canal House	28	Putnam County Court House
3	DeWint House	27	Rokeby
5	DuBois Fort	41	Rossiter House
31	Edgewater	18	Schuyler Mansion
9	Edmonston House	21	Senate House
45	Estherwood	32	Springwood
35	Jacob Blauvelt House	36	Sunnyside
16	Knox Headquarters	24	Ten Broeck House
23	Lindenwald	15	Van Cortlandt Manor
34	Locust Grove	48	Vanderbilt Mansion
37	Lyndhurst	30	Vanderpoel House
6	Madam Brett Homestead	7	Van Deusen House
40	The Malcolm Gordon School	13	Van Wyck Homestead
17	Mandeville House	8	Washington's Headquarters
11	The Manse	39	Wilderstein

HUDSON RIVER VALLEY

Tappan
DeWint House
The Manse

New City
Jacob Blauvelt House

Vails Gate
Edmonston House
Knox Headquarters

New Windsor
New Windsor Cantonment

Newburgh
Crawford House
Washington's Headquarters

New Paltz
DuBois Fort
Mohonk Mountain House

High Falls
DePuy Canal House

Hurley
Van Deusen House

Kingston
Senate House

Catskill
Cedar Grove

Albany
Albany City Hall
New York State Capitol
Schuyler Mansion
Ten Broeck House

Rhinebeck
Delamater House
Wilderstein

Red Hook
Edgewater
Rokeby

Annandale
Blithewood
Montgomery Place

Germantown
Clermont

Kinderhook
Lindenwald
Vanderpoel House

Rensselaer
Crailo

Beacon
Bannerman's Castle
Madam Brett Homestead
Mount Gulian

Fishkill
Van Wyck Homestead

Poughkeepsie
Clinton House
Locust Grove

Hyde Park
Springwood
Vanderbilt Mansion

Staatsburg
Mills Mansion

Croton
Van Cortlandt Manor

Garrison
Boscobel
The Malcolm Gordon School
Mandeville House

Cold Spring
Rossiter House

Carmel
Putnam County Court House

Tarrytown
Lyndhurst
Sunnyside

North Tarrytown
Old Dutch Church
Philipsburg Manor

Yonkers
Philipse Manor Hall

Dobbs Ferry
Estherwood

ARTIST'S BIOGRAPHY

Karl Beckwith Smith III was born in Saranac Lake, New York, in 1950. He studied art history at Princeton University and made an extended tour of Europe and its museums in 1973. In 1983, after ten years of life in a lower Manhattan loft, he moved to Cold Spring and established Stencilsmith, a decorative painting company specializing in stenciling, marbleizing, gilding, murals, antique restoration and interior and furniture decoration. Decorative commissions led to artistic commissions and, finally, to the opportunity to work full time as an artist.

Smith's first one-man show was held in May 1988 at Turn of the Century in Cold Spring. His current work in pen and ink wash is an outgrowth of the Cold Spring drawings exhibited at that show. Smith also works in watercolor and oil.

In the course of researching the art and architecure of the Hudson River Valley, Smith has discovered his descendancy from artist Gerardus Duyckinck (circa 1695-1746) and three generations of early Albany Dutch decorative painters.

ACKNOWLEDGEMENTS

A project like this one does not come to fruition and to the attention of the public without a great deal of effort from many people. To the following people I extend my deepest thanks for the part each has played in making my dream a reality:
Mary Kay Vrba, Hudson River Valley Association; Cynthia Grant; Montgomery Place; Elizabeth Dale Crary, Albany City Hall; Robert Pucci and Billy Name, Mid-Hudson Art & Science Center; Gerry Baldwin, Alice and Hamilton Fish Library; Sarah Edwards-Clarke, Southeast Museum; Niel Larson, Dutchess County Historical Society.

For their help in producing the book thanks to Charlotte Krebs and Ruth Eisenhower.

For their special support and encouragement I would like to thank Karen Dunn and Frederick Stanyer, Boscobel Restoration; Gail Greet Hannah and Caroline Krebs, Salmagundi Press; Rosemarie and Ed Cretelli, Jake Cretelli and Susan Early, C&E Paint.

And for his unique contribution, thanks to Hal H. Truesdale.

K.B.S. III